CONCILIUM

CONCILIUM 2021/3

Incarnation in a Post/Human Age

Edited by

Susan Abraham, Bernardeth Caero Bustillos, and Po Ho Huang

Published in 2021 by SCM Press, 3rd Floor, Invicta House, 108–114 Golden Lane, London, EC1Y 0TG.

SCM Press is an imprint of Hymns Ancient & Modern Ltd (a registered charity) 13A Hellesdon Park Road, Norwich NR6 5DR, UK

www.concilium.in

ISBN 978-0-334-03159-8

Printed in the UK by
Ashford, Hampshire

Concilium is published in March, June, August, October, December

Contents

Editorial

Do "The Incarnation" and "Incarnational Theology," which are central aspects of Christian thought have resonance and relevance in a Post/Human Age? Post/Human is Elaine Graham's elegant solution bridging two separate discourses: Posthumanism and Transhumanism.[1] Both posthumanism and transhumanism are inaugurated in the context of what Graham calls the "technologization of nature." Human beings now think of life as a "flow of information," that can be downloaded or uploaded as the case requires, into other than carbon-based life forms, as portrayed in popular culture like film and video games. The blurring of boundaries between humanity, technology and nature creates deep questions for ontology and theological anthropology even as such yearnings for transcendence rekindle a religious and theological imagination. To many, the emphasis on technology and information compromises the Christian understanding of the incarnation and the incarnational theology that flows from it. Others see an opportunity for a more complex engagement for theological and religious imaginations.

Such religious and theological imaginations are evident in the essays collected in this volume. Authors in Part 1 offer philosophical perspectives on contemporary discussions of posthumanism. Elaine Graham's essay explores the possibility of transgressing the borders between immanence and transcendence, secular and sacred, humanity and divinity in a dialogue between critical posthumanism and cyborg identities. Philip Butler provides another perspective through his salient analysis of "race" and discourses of post/humanism. His essay argues that Black African Americans and Black people have always been "post" human since their very humanity has been erased in Eurocentric discourses, including discourses of liberation. Finally, Stefan Sorgner's essay argues that the idea of religious leisure, that is, the contemplation of God, cannot be separated from an incarnational frame for posthumanism.

In Part 2, the authors explore aspects of popular culture and posthumanism. Heidi Campbell traces how narratives about posthumanism are influencing the arguments being made by religious groups dependent on technology during COVID-19, sounding a note of caution on such retrievals, which could compromise the theological and incarnational in religious discourses. Andrea Vicini similarly questions the posthuman moral agent, asking if their unquestioned trust in technology and its promises are justified, especially when evaluating the losses of embodiment and incarnational ethics in posthumanism. In contrast, Susan Abraham argues that popular narratives about posthumanism, best seen in the Unites States culture in Superhero comics and films are imaginative constructions about the post/human, but narratives in which American social issues like race and gender press on normative ideas about the human. Black superhero films in such a view challenge the racism and sexism of both popular cultural imaginations of the human and post/human.

Part 3 turns explicitly to the problems posed by cyber-reality. The authors here are not in agreement about the extent to which cyber-reality "disincarnates." Jeanine Thweatt-Bates for example, in a specifically feminist vein challenges the notion that the presumed "technognosticism" of the upload scenario in many post/human analyses avoids the problem of specific embodiment by focusing on disembodiment. In so doing, her analysis draws lines of continuity with Butler's essay in Part 1 and Abraham's essay in Part 2. Jay Johnson's essay provides another interesting tack. Starting from the explicitly theological and incarnational logic of the Real Presence of Christ in the Eucharist, Johnson explores the impact of disembodied liturgies and the possibility of disincarnation in the time of COVID-19 on our sense of communion, asserting that when the carnal possibility of communion is denied, the Eucharist must be celebrated eschatologically, a vital echo of Vatican II. Raúl Fornet-Betancourt presents a strong argument against the idea that post/humanism is an improvement of the human being and asserts that human mortality is of great value to the human condition. Betancourt therefore, asserts that with the Incarnation of the Logos, "flesh" is a place of theophany and a site of continuing gratitude for human beings. Lee Cormie conversely, tracks the emergence of transhumanism, posthumanism and Anthropocene as "epochal transitions" in the life of our planet, asserting that we are witnessing the birth of a completely different time for our species including the possibility of its end. Finally, H. S. Wilson argues for a renewed commitment to Christian theology as human beings continue to build Artificial Intelligence with greater capacity.

The authors in this issue's Forum focus on the following: Paul M. Zulehner addresses the theme of various forms of priesthood vis-à-vis new realities lived in the world Church, such as the growing shortage of priests. As he writes: "This is why the Amazon Synod struggled and made proposals to the Pope. The Pope decided not to decide". Geraldina Cespedes sets out the four dreams put forward by Pope Francis in his apostolic exhortation "Dear Amazonia": A Church that dreams again; a Social Dream: the rights of the poorest; a Cultural Dream: preserving biodiversity, and an Ecological Dream: taking care of our Common Home. Taking as a starting point the reality of the Black Lives Matter movement, Lucas Cerviño deals with the subject of otherness and violence on the American continent. The author indicates that the non-recognition of diversity is a denial of the God who is Communion.

Susan Abraham, Bernardeth Caero and Po Ho Huang

Notes

1. Elaine Graham, *Representations of the Post/Human: Monsters, Aliens and Others in Popular Culture* (New Brunswick, New Jersey: Rutgers University Press), 2002.

Part One: Philosophical Perspectives

The Spiritual Cyborg: Religion and Posthumanism from Secular to Postsecular

ELAINE GRAHAM

This article works on the premise that critical posthumanism exposes and calls into question the criteria by which Western modernity has defined the boundaries between nature, humanity, and technology. The religious, cultural and epistemological developments of what is known as the "postsecular" may signal a blurring of another set of distinctions characteristic of modernity: those between sacred and secular, belief and non-belief. Using Donna Haraway's famous assertion that she would "rather be a cyborg than a goddess", I will consider whether critical posthumanism in the form of cyborg identities is also capable of tracing, and crossing, this "final frontier" between immanence and transcendence, secular and sacred, humanity and divinity.

I Introduction

In *A Manifesto for Cyborgs* Donna Haraway famously declared, "I would rather be a cyborg than a goddess."[1] This has been a matter of debate and analysis ever since. Her advocacy of the figure of the cyborg has been hugely influential across a range of disciplines considering the impact of advanced technologies on culture and society, including feminist theory, cultural studies and philosophy of technology. In its defiance of fixed organic essences, the cyborg represents the transgression of species and category boundaries (human/machine, nature/culture, biological/cybernetic) thereby becoming the symbol for the rejection of race, gender or species essentialism, or any totalizing identity. It is a "*myth* about transgressed boundaries, potent fusions, and dangerous possibilities".[2] As a hybrid, fluid pastiche of parts, the cyborg embodies "the promises of monsters"[3] and represents a call to find liberation in identities that are hybrid, fluid and inter-connected.

In this article, I want to return specifically to the binary opposition between cyborg and goddess in Haraway's essay. This has intrigued me and other scholars, especially in the study of religion, for many years.[4] In the context of an essay that celebrates augmented bodies, hybrid identities and complex affinities, and which has been a foundational text for the discipline known as critical posthumanism, how are we to "read" Haraway's statement of what appears to be a form of dualism? Does it represent a rejection of a particular kind of theological thinking that associates divinity with an immutable, dispassionate deity in whose image humanity yearns for disembodied "transcendence"? Or the repudiation of a traditional, matriarchal imagined past in favour of a futuristic anthropology of technologized hybridity? What is she saying in expressing a preference for one over the other; and what can be learned about how we might locate religion, theology and the sacred – including understandings of incarnation and personhood – in the light of that? In essence: is there space for a religious dimension to such a posthuman vision?

II The Secular Cyborg

Certainly, there is a strong affinity between modern technoscience and a broadly secular, rationalist perspective in which religion and science, belief and scepticism, theism and atheism are regarded as incompatible opposites. Haraway's dichotomy makes some sense within the prevailing secular and materialist emphasis of contemporary science and technology studies and feminist theory, which regards adoption of advanced technologies and celebration of human affinity with nature and technology as diametrically opposed to an imagined religious world-view of fixed essences and a hierarchy of body/spirit. It also represents a rejection of essentialized, "God-given" limitations on human potential. There is an assumption, therefore, that posthumanism, both in its critical and transhumanist varieties, will be far removed from the concerns of religion.

Nevertheless, there are also significant ways in which religion features within discourses and representations of posthumanism. This reflects the emergence of what some would call a "postsecular" culture, in which new and enduring forms of religiosity co-exist with enduring secular and atheist world-views. Within a postsecular paradigm, it might be possible to regard religion as *both* inimical to scientific progress and human advancement *and* as the source of ancient wisdom that continues to inform understandings of what it means to be human – and by extension, posthuman.

To read the cyborg and the goddess through such an alternative, postsecular lens, then, is to be invited to reintroduce the sacred into contemporary social theory. In defiance of the trajectories of secularization and the mind-set of secularism, therefore, we find ourselves transgressing not only the ontological boundaries of humanity, nature and technology but crossing the "final frontier" between religion and the sacred. It is a matter, initially, of thinking "genealogically"[5] about the way both posthuman and postsecular have their origins in the critique of the assumptions that shaped Western modernity. These were to do with the elevation of the human subject as autonomous and self-determining, distinguished from animals, nature and machines; and as uniquely rational and unconstrained by the bounds of superstition, tradition and religion.

In one branch of posthumanism, the philosophy of transhumanism, we see a thoroughly expansive embrace of technology that is unambiguously at the service of the ambitions of modern, Western humanist philosophy. Transhumanism is premised on an embrace of radical Enlightenment humanism, in which new technologies continue to facilitate the continued evolution of the human species whose abiding characteristic rests in its inventive, rational instinct for invention and self-enhancement.[6] According to this vision, human enhancement does not threaten true personhood, on the basis that it is actually an extension of our "essential" qualities of rationality, autonomy and self-improvement. Transhumanism challenges any notion of limitation or boundedness to human biology and positions *natural* and *technological* as diametrically opposed concepts. The latter serves as the solution to the problems of finitude, entropy and risk that arise from the former. As a "standing reserve", nature is an entirely legitimate object of human scrutiny and manipulation; and "transcendence" of culture over nature is an expression of the ontological and moral distance between humanity and other species. Yet as I shall argue, even within this expansive embrace of technologized humanity there is space for religion.

By contrast, an alternative strand known as critical posthumanism positions itself in relation to an understanding of human ontology that is altogether more contested. It denotes "a general critical space" in which the "stability of the categories 'human' and 'nonhuman' can be called into question".[7]

If posthumanism is humanity imagined beyond the paradigm of humanism, then it also highlights the genetic and ecological continuum of human and non-human nature, the malleability of genetic and digital technologies, the ubiquity of virtual and computer-mediated communications and their accompanying influence on our altered experiences of space, place, community and embodiment. It means that the biological and the technological, the material (or "real") and the virtual are co-existent and co-evolving. The inability to disentangle everyday life from its (inter) dependence upon or with advanced technologies renders the classical humanist subject obsolete.

Posthuman has become a way of naming the unknown, possible, (perhaps) future, altered identity of human beings, as we incorporate various technologies into our human bodies and selves. It therefore functions as an umbrella term, covering a span of related concepts: genetically enhanced persons, artificial persons or androids, uploaded consciousnesses, cyborgs and chimeras (mechanical or genetic hybrids). Thus, the posthuman is not any one particular thing; it is an act of projection, of speculation about who we are as human beings, and who we might become.[8]

Thus, talk of the posthuman is a way of tracing the processes and discourses by which we have differentiated organic from inorganic, nature from artefact, human from non-human. To ascribe the prefix "post" is to highlight that these categories are a construction or artefact, and to recognize the porosity of the boundaries between the human, non-human and "otherwise human".[9] The posthuman represents a refusal to fix or reify human nature or essence independent of an account of humanity's co-evolution with its environments, tools and artefacts.

In speaking about the ascendancy of modern humanism, Bruno Latour has argued that it was premised on "the simultaneous birth of 'nonhumanity' – things, or objects, or beasts – *and* the equally strange beginning of a *crossed-out God*, relegated to the side-lines."[10] Latour's reference to theology gestures towards another constituent in the emergence of modernity: the birth of a discrete philosophy, or sphere of life, known as the "secular". The creation of an autonomous, self-actualizing humanity was as dependent on the suppression of the transcendent, the divine non-human, as it was on the creation of a binary opposition between the normatively human and its "others" in nature, the animal kingdom or in the world of tools, technologies and machines. Yet if an investigation into the genealogy of humanism reveals its roots in the establishment of certain material and discursive boundaries associated with the birth of Western modernity, then we are led inevitably to another set of ontological and epistemological fault-lines: those which demarcate secularity from religion, matter from metaphysics, reason from superstition.

III Beyond Secularism

Jürgen Habermas' work has been closely associated with the "postsecular" turn in social theory and political philosophy, initially as a way of accounting for the resurgence of religion as a political force in global civil society at the end of the twentieth century.[11] Despite the predictions of secularization theory, religion has not vanished from the public domain. This is apparent not only in the global resurgence of religiously-motivated activism, in Christianity, Islam, or Hinduism, but also in the persistence of heterodox forms of personal spirituality, including those who report themselves to be "Spiritual but not Religious" or in the renewed interest in forms of theological and Biblical scholarship among contemporary philosophers.

Part of the complexity of the postsecular, however, is that it does not attempt to deny the functionally secular nature of much of Western society. Despite the "new visibility" of religion over the past thirty years, none of this represents a reversal of secularization and certainly not a reversion to pre-modern or theocratic paradigms of medicine, politics, gender roles, cosmology and so on. The decline in the cultural influence of and formal affiliation to organized religion is undeniable; and in public life there is continued and vigorous resistance to admitting any legitimacy for religion within the realms of politics, law, education, and morality. The postsecular is, therefore, more an acknowledgement of the "simultaneous … decline, mutation and resurgence"[12] of religious believing and belonging.

The postsecular is positioned, then, at the interface of the renewed or continuing presence of religion, spirituality and the sacred, and the political settlements and epistemological legacies of secularism, materialism, and humanism. Just as the postsecular describes a situation in which modernity and postmodernity, secular and religious co-exist as overlapping and conflicting paradigms, however, we can perhaps begin to see how religion and the sacred have never been entirely absent from versions of the *posthuman*, either.

IV The Spiritual Cyborg

Alongside the discourse of humanist and transhumanist self-actualization, there has always been evidence of an attitude to technologies as the realization of (particular kinds of) metaphysical and spiritual endeavours. Erik Davis has argued that a supposedly post-religious modernity has not succeeded in eliminating "occult dreamings, spiritual transformations, and apocalyptic visions". Instead, they "went underground, worming their way into the cultural, psychological, and mythological motivations that form the foundations of the modern world."[13] Advanced technologies appear invested with a quasi-magical and mystical power, which "embodies an image of the soul, or rather a host of images: redemptive, demonic, magical, transcendent, hypnotic, alive."[14] There are intriguing parallels between humanity's technological endeavours and a kind of demiurgical instinct – to become gods, to ascend to the heavens, to abandon the "meat" of human embodiment in order to attain a virtual, immortal existence.

Similarly, movements such as transhumanism foresee a world in which digital, cybernetic, genetic and biomedical technologies become the instruments of the next phase of human evolution, whereby *homo sapiens* will mutate into *homo cyberneticus* or *techno sapiens*. This draws a clear analogy between technologically-facilitated enhancement of human limitation and the assumption of superhuman, god-like powers, to the extent that transhumanism begins to resemble a New Religious Movement, complete with charismatic leaders, sacred texts and carefully-delineated eschatology of human perfectibility and *theosis*. Clearly, then, even in a supposedly secular age, expressions of religion continue to fuel our technological ambitions and our visions of the ends to which advanced technologies might transport us.

V Cyborg/Goddess

We return, therefore, to Donna Haraway, to discover whether it is possible to make a postsecular reading of her preference for cyborgs over the goddess. It encourages us to look for the ways in which the after-life of traditional religion and its mutations function within Haraway's work. We discover how she embodies some of the contradictions and complexities of the postsecular, not least by describing herself as anti-Catholic while drawing on vivid Christian symbolism. For example, in her playful allusions to the Genesis creation and Fall narratives in *Manifesto*, the vision of cyborg posthumanity is not one of nostalgia for fixed essences, a loss of innocence "about the Fall, the imagination of a once-upon-a-time wholeness",[15] but about the formation of an inclusive, ethical, planetary coalition of species at ease with their own ontological ambivalence. The cyborg is Haraway's "ironic faith, my blasphemy"[16] inviting heretical thought-experiments beyond the heterodoxies of patriarchy and industrial-capitalism. In another essay, OncoMouse™, a genetically modified laboratory mouse transplanted with an oncogene for the purposes of breast cancer research, assumes a Christlike redemptive significance, complete with crown of thorns and allusions to the Biblical motif of the suffering servant.

In that respect, Haraway's "Catholic sacramentalism" or "sacramental materiality"[17] as a strategy of resistance to dualism is significant. "Haraway's resistance to the separation of the material and the semiotic can be seen as the philosophical result of a sacramentalism that accepts the material instantiation of the symbolic and sacred."[18] In the sacrament, the sacred suffuses the material which is the means, or medium, and sign of divine grace. It serves to re-unite matter and spirit, nature and agency, transcendence and incarnation. The boundaries of material and metaphysical, sacred and secular, are themselves dissolved. Divinity re-enchants the material, technological world, as well as natural/non-human ecologies and environments by means of a "radical immanence and raw cosmic power"[19] that dissolves the (false) dichotomies of secular modernity.

The effect, then, of reclaiming the goddess in the context of critical posthumanism is to effect a move to a post-metaphysical theology in which the binaries of transcendent/immanent, sacred/secular, spiritual/material are deconstructed. In the process, the figure of the goddess challenges the heretical, patriarchal God and secular modernist understandings of material, embodied, and temporal existence as devoid of sacrality. Just as postsecularity challenges the ontological and epistemological separation of religion from the rest of our lived experience, so sacramentalism locates divinity, the sacred, and transcendence as a part of, not apart from, culture, technology, and ethics.

If there is no need to place cyborgs and goddesses on opposite sides of a material/metaphysical ontology, then the way is clear to consider their affinities rather than their differences. Far from inhabiting separate universes, goddess and cyborg share similar monstrous, hybrid, and transgressive ontologies. Both challenge the ontological hygiene of humanity-nature-technology; and both demonstrate the epiphanic potential of posthuman and divine "others" to subvert reductionist accounts of those same categories.

VI Conclusion

Just as critical posthumanism points to the artifice of our own identity in relation to nature, culture, and technology, so the return of religion to the cultural imaginary requires us to reconsider the shifting fault-lines of dis/enchantment. The postsecular represents an opportunity to rethink those binaries and, like critical posthumanism, to conceive of human personhood and community beyond the categories imposed by secular modernity. If the posthuman alerts us to the contingency of the boundaries by which we separate the human from the non-human, the technological from the biological, artificial from natural, then the postsecular questions the fixity of the boundary between science and religion, profane and sacred and modernity's evacuation of faith from accepted conventions of public and moral reasoning.

By adopting a postsecular perspective, then, we can read Haraway's iconic statement as a way of rejecting Western modernist traditions of divine transcendence that divide the spiritual from the material – including the discourse of secularism – in favour of a future which acknowledges the affinities between the "human, non-human, and more-than-human".[20] In the context of the re-enchanted realms of technology, nature and cosmos it provides a renewed theological anthropology and ecology for the pursuit of a more integrated and sustainable vision of planetary living.

Notes

1. Donna Haraway, "A Cyborg Manifesto: Science, Technology, and Socialist-Feminism in the Late Twentieth Century," in D.J. Haraway (ed.), *Simians, Cyborgs and Women: The Reinvention of Nature,* London: Free Association Books, 149-182, here 181.
2. Haraway, "Manifesto," 154, my emphasis.
3. Donna Haraway, "The Promises of Monsters: a Regenerative Politics for Inappropriate/d Others," in The Haraway Reader, London: Routledge, 2004, 63-124.
4. Elaine Graham, *Representations of the Post/Human*, Manchester: Manchester University Press, 2002; Nina Lykke, "To Be a Cyborg or a Goddess?" *Gender, Technology and Development* 1.1 (1997), 5-22; Ruth Mantin, "A Thealogy of Radical Immanence: Goddess and the Posthuman," *Feminist Theology* (2019), 6-19; Scott Midson, *Cyborg Theology: Humans, Technology and God*, London: I.B. Tauris, 2018; Jeanine Thweatt-Bates, *Cyborg Selves: A Theological Anthropology of the Posthuman*, Farnham: Ashgate, 2012.
5. Talal Asad, *Formations of the Secular: Christianity, Islam*, Modernity. Stanford, CA: Stanford University Press, 2003.
6. Nick Bostrom, "A History of Transhuman Thought," J*ournal of Evolution and Technology*, 14.1 (2005), 1-25. For a critical perspective on humanism and technology, see Taner Edis, "Technological Progress and Pious Modernity: Secular Liberals Fall Behind the Times,", in Anthony B. Pinn (ed.), *Humanism and Technology: Opportunities and Challenges*, New York: Palgrave Macmillan, 2016, 123-142.
7. Catherine Waldby, *The Visible Human Project: Informatic Bodies and Posthuman Medicine*, London: Routledge, 2000, 43.
8. Thweatt-Bates, *Cyborg Selves*, 1.
9. Rosi Braidotti, *The Posthuman*, Cambridge: Polity, 2013, 196.
10. Bruno Latour, *We Have Never Been Modern*, Cambridge, MA: Harvard University Press, 1993, 13, my emphasis.
11. Jürgen Habermas et al. (eds.), *An Awareness of what is Missing: Faith and Reason in a Post-Secular Age*, Cambridge: Polity, 2010.
12. Elaine Graham, *Between a Rock and a Hard Place: Public Theology in a Post-Secular Age*, London: SCM Press, 2013, 3.
13. Erik Davis, *Techgnosis: Myth, Magic and Mysticism in the Age of Information*, London: Serpent's Tail, 1998, 2-3.
14. Davis, Techgnosis, 9.
15. Haraway "Manifesto," 175.
16. "Manifesto," 149.
17. Thyrza Nichols Goodeve, How Like a Leaf: An Interview with Donna Haraway, London: Routledge, 2000, 24; Thweatt-Bates, *Cyborg Selves,* 83.
18. Thweatt-Bates, *Cyborg Selves*, 82.
19. Mantin, "Thealogy of Radical Immanence," 19.

Blackness: Spectres and Monsters are the Future of Theological Subjectivity

PHILIP BUTLER

*This essay peers into the off-centred points of globality in hopes to unpack a few nodes of posthuman subjectivity—namely Blackness. Historically, the ghostly and monstrous were used to distance Blackness from the humanity and divinity. Outside of the realm of Black theology, Blackness has not historically been associated with divine embodiment/incarnation. This essay seeks to turn the terms spectre and monster on their head, being subjectivities that bear divine reality. An investigation into the dangers posed by Black spectral and monstrous divinity points toward new posthuman subjectivities (*being *spectres and monsters of Black personhood and divinity).*

Whenever people see a ghost, they make sense of it the best they know how. Or not. Very little prepares people for seeing a ghost, except experience with the ghostly. Further, people rarely actually see the spectre. They see and feel the effects the ghost's interactions with their environment.[1] The same goes for making sense of an encounter with a monster. What is worse, experiencing the divine is no different. The ineffable/unspeakable aspects of divine encounters often leave people with a sense of awe that is primarily perceptible through the effects of said encounter. Where one might say, "I had an encounter with God," or "God moved on my behalf." It often follows that whatever people encounter immediately becomes transcribed through the epistemological nodes upholding their historically situated sense of self/reality. These transcriptions serve to bolster the stability of their phenomenological experience. Thus, people seldomly see beyond the spectres/phantoms of their own imagination. This essay peers into the off-centred points of globality to unpack a few aspects of posthuman subjectivity—namely Black bodies/biotechnology through the ghostly and monstrous.[2] Traditionally, posthuman subjects are complex and pluralized. To date posthuman subjects have ranged from quantum foam entities to the Black posthuman transformer.[3] In each instance posthuman subjects are examples of existence outside, beyond, or in opposition to the primary subject of rational humanism. Here, Black bodies function as posthuman subjectivities which act oppositionally and exist in ways that threaten to shatter/demolish/undo the existence/maintenance/persistence of humanistic sensibilities/realities. An exploration of these metaphoric descriptors, specifically in relation to the danger they pose to white supremacist realities, might allow for a lens to surface which points toward posthuman subjectivities of the future (*being* the spectres and monsters of Black personhood and divinity).

I Kids See Ghosts Sometimes

Seeing a spectre/phantom/ghost is reminiscent of when the white child discovered Frantz Fanon in public and exclaimed in excitement/terror "Look! A Negro!"[4] The child saw the Black male spectre and surprised at its appearance, made a pronouncement – as if to ensure other people saw it as well. It suggests the child had heard of the Black male spectre, but seeing it provided a sense of material manifestation to all that was learned. Moreover, what Fanon alludes to, are the effects of his appearance in the middle of white society; the social tension and weight of existential angst that surfaces bi-directionally. Although most presciently through white-behaviour when white people realize Black people actually exist. A most heart-wrenching example of the Black female spectre is the case of Breonna Taylor who was murdered by members of the Louisville Metro Police Department. In the grand jury decision, the only indictment announced was in relation to the bullets that went through her wall and into her neighbour's home. The six bullets that entered her body, killing her, were not accounted for in the decision. It was as if she was not there, making either her death a mystery, her life a mystery, or the events that night the expected/justifiable effects of police encounters with spectres of Black embodiment. This also speaks to the invisibilization of Black women that extends through death. As ghosts, Black female spectres are rendered unaccounted for, reinforcing nonexistence, another effect of inhabiting the realm of phantoms. The effects of her presence were the shielding of her neighbour's walls from further bullet penetration. These events are etched in historically rendered documents, maintained in the annals of American mythology.

White supremacy has functioned, and continues to function, as a broad epistemic framework of western european imperial structures.[5] It intentionally negates the Black post-/antihuman. White supremacy's persistence in present and future societies has, and will be, tied to the manner in which its post-colonial sites/descendants hold firmly to the comfort embedded within its assumptions, power and privilege.[6] Cognitive science and phenomenological studies combine to affirm similar stances; people's perceptions are formed by their culture, thoughts, and bodies.[7] Further, classical theology and its anthropological tentacles have consistently been more concerned with extending humanistic sensibilities. Cloaked in the medium of religious scholarship, rational humanism's dedication to stratified value systems makes it apparent that within theological anthropology the human in question is not a member of the global majority. Extensive analysis has already been conducted on preeminent works by scholars such as Kant, Hume, Hegel, or Rahner which often expressed intentional disinterest in exploring the relationship between multivariate being/existence and the multitudinal expression of divinity. Their ghosts continue to linger in humanism's mutations (post-structuralism, post-colonialism, feminism, transhumanism, posthumanism, etc.).

In the genres of horror and posthumanity the monster and the spectre are simultaneously unavoidable and indestructible. However, from the perspective of western european vantage points nothing properly exists outside the realm/limitations of the human. Humberto Maturana argues that reality is the chief problem of relational existence.[8] Objectivity, being the result of observable, reiterable experience grounds all references points/bodies in reality. This also points to the exaggerated emphasis on relativity in terms of objectivity. Here, Maturana delineates between objectivity within and without parenthesis. Objectivity-within-parenthesis (OWiP) gives account for hyper-subjectivity, hyper relativity, and the significance/worth of the perspective of the individual subject. Objectivity-without-parenthesis (OWoP) is more closely aligned with the singular reality prescribed by european thinkers of modern settler colonialism. The point is that one makes spectres of anything outside its fixed/static system (OWoP) while the other gives room for any, and all, existent possibilities, claiming no point of exception over other potential materializations of reality (OWiP). In the case of objectivity-within-parentheses, a multiverse or a pluriverse are more than feasible co-evolving potentialities.[9] In these multidimensional planes, nothing would be considered outside the realm of existence. While the pluriversal potential for infinite dimensions and planes of existence are fun conceptual tools to play with, I think it will be more fruitful to attempt to expand the singular objectivity-without-parentheses perspective via the designations of spectres and monsters. Precisely because neither can be avoided or destroyed in the genres of horror and posthumanity. Further the subject/object of aversion, fear and ominous aboding often wins in the aforementioned genres/realities.

II Grotesquery, or the Monstrous

The state of the grotesque situates Black posthuman existence in relationship with the end/destruction of the "[hu]man."[10] In Victor Anderson's *Beyond Ontological Blackness* the grotesque becomes the node of meaning attached to Black biotechnologies, affixed within the realm of the ghost/spectre or monster.[11] Here, Black posthumans, as monsters and ghosts, speak to the way Black bodies are simultaneously overemphasized and disincarnate. Disincarnate beings, whose acknowledged physical presence is monstrous or fleeting, often experience totally different realities than humans. In the case of Blackness this has often ended fatally—as physical disincarnation from the body (either through social death, genocide, or homicide). The grotesque body is often rendered as sudden and devoid of physical presence (disincarnate spectre), or as boding and ominous physicality (disincarnate monster). Grotesque bodies are marginalized, made invisible, yet hyper-visible, and stripped of any sense of belonging or safety. Even within traditional posthuman subjectivities. Critical, philosophical, ecological, gendered and even "hintedly" racialized posthumanisms still project "acceptable"/respectable/safe and universalistic approaches to what may be considered generatively posthuman.[12] Even more so, ideas suggesting decentrality of the human by humans provide a sense of being situated as always human until no longer human. It also presupposes the concreteness of "the human" as progenitor of all existence without fully exploring, or naming, the human as a fantastical assemblage of stolen legacies and white supremacist colonial mythologies.

In the grander scheme of biopolitical framings of power, privilege and mobility/freedom, each often skews toward a sliding scale of necropolitics, debility, or any other centring of "humans", who are nonhuman human animals (usually labelled human animals).[13] As a conceptual node, nonhuman human animal speaks to the myriad ways humanity operates as an ontology employed to order universal frameworks. However, it is in no way indicative of the embodied psychologies that bear its designation. In essence, the nonhuman human animal is the marker for protonormative whiteness historically elevated to the status of human. It very pointedly declares that white people are not even human. Still, in the context of human discourse of any ilk, Black bodies are considered grotesque. Grotesque bodies exist in the realm of the monstrous, where discarnate bodies are not given credible existence because subscribers to objectivity-without-parentheses make monsters out of anything outside known aspects of singular universalities. However, Black posthumanity exists at the other side of both, fully-embodied. Reveling in the ashes and rubble left in the wake of the human's apocalypse.

III Mining the Galaxy for Monsters and Meaning

When physicists cannot describe the fabric of the universe the weight of the unknown is labelled with the descriptor of "dark". New unknowns mark segments of existence yet to be understood as dark spaces of reality. Here, darkness represents posthuman knowledge, existing beyond the limits of human comprehension. Monsters are dark creatures. They represent the grotesque and unknown elements of embodiment that readily illicit anxiety in human psyches. They are morphologically exaggerated, with characteristics attributed to deities, the elements, or super-/metahumans. Human perceptions disincarnate the actuality of what/who is before them, narrowly focusing on the abstract elements of embodiment which inspire awe and initiate the fear response. In this way, the superhuman is simultaneously subhuman and monster, but always more than human.

The overman, or transhuman, has served as a posthuman edifice from which to progress humanity—physically, spirituality, intellectually, etc.[14] The overman is a Nietzschean term, but I think Nietzsche was imagining Black people. Harriet Washington's Medical Apartheid demonstrates that western medicine's physical archetype of biological existence is Black.[15] Even more so, Marquis Bey argues in "Between Blackness and Monstrosity" that "the monster is often seen most pervasively in . . . arenas dominated by Black subjects . . . [and] is redeployed as a desirable characterization insofar as it denotes the subject's otherworldliness and ability to do things mere humans cannot."[16] So, outside appropriate arenas superhumans/monsters are constantly short changed. More specifically the superhuman is rendered invisible for its utility, while the monster is granted hyper-visibility for its menacing potential. Superhuman utility disassociates Black bodies from their movements (in white gazes), whereas monstrosity makes the body and its actions very easy to pinpoint/police. The superhuman is a god, a spectre/spirit, and a miracle while the monster embodies the very essence of what the human fears a god, or otherworldly entity, might do in physical form. Still the superhuman/monster remains the designated archetype for human evolution—physically, intellectually and spiritually.

The existence of monsters destabilizes what was once thought to be a static/fixed reality. Fixedness speaks more to its seemingly autopoietic (self-replicating) qualities. Moreover, that would also presuppose some larger stable system orchestrating the entire present reality. While many might like to think there is an overarching cosmological umbrella keeping everything together, we are learning that dynamicity, or infinite variability, is more likely the case. This does not mean nothing exists. It soberly suggests that what is will not always be in the state it once was. What is more, physicists are becoming more aware that there is no final/ultimate theory to encapsulate the functioning of the universe. In contrast, Infinite variability might be among the closest thing to that which is holding everything together. Consequently, instability would substitute any notion of stability. If infinite variability were, in fact, the closest to what might be considered an overarching understanding of the universe then this infinite variability might be closer to a lesser ascribed to notion concerning divinity. Here, "I am that I am" (as a static anchor in a fixed reality) meets

"I will be what I will be" or "I will be whatever I create"—as a variable representation of a fluctuating reality.[17] Instability suggests behind any notion of certainty lies myth, lore and uncertainty. In addition, this calls into question any previous concrete offerings of divine embodiment. Further, myth leads to some form of inaccuracy, mirage or imaginary. When such mirages/inaccuracies lead to disproportionately distributed value in personhood or relationality to reify hierarchy/stratification one could argue there is intention to deceive. Intentional deceit in a society grounded in myth is what Aimé Césaire calls a "dying civilization"; a one-way road to Hitler.[18] Two layers of the previous statement need peeling back: intentionality and myth. Intentional deceit being attached to a society suggests that society is grounded in an intended telos regardless of any impact said telos has on its citizens. Similarly, mythology can be a synonym for reality or epistemology, given the manner epistemologies employ unknown or lesser-known elements/nodes as fillers for knowledge. If knowledge is mined/excavated, or unfolding, over time this suggests whatever people hold to be the case today is mere myth compared to what may be discovered tomorrow. Adding to Césaire, an intentionally deceitful society, equippcd with supporting theolog(ies) and epistemolog(ies) is a dying reality. Dying societies rooted in the mythos of white supremacy are on a one-way road to culturally embodying the religion of white supremacy. Césaire further notes that acts committed to maintain and spread "civilization" simultaneously are categorized as barbaric. The cultural embodiment of the religion of white supremacy moves societies from processes of dying into the death of that society.

IV A Different Social Death

Afropessimism defines social death as the total irredeemable nonbeing/non-humanity of Blackness in sociality, the result of a haunting/lingering systematically imposed anti-Black violence. As mentioned above, social death carries disincarnating qualities. In contrast, here, social death is the death of a society whose foundation is white supremacy. This kind of social death leads to the death/disincarnation of its presupposed reality, where rotting nodes give away to entropy/destabilization/death. Releasing said society, and its myths, into nearby dimensions where the spectres and monsters (formerly designated as nonbeings) are most visible: In the land of the spectres and monsters. That is where once avoidable and seemingly glimpsing entities are most tangible, lucid and powerful. In the land of the spectres and monsters, a space Ebony Elizabeth Thomas calls the "Dark Fantastic,"[19] new inhabitants often find that the mythical/wild/mad qualities ascribed to spectres and monsters are true. However, in the land of spectres and monsters the veneer of previous virtual existences are disrupted, ruptured, and turned on their head. At that very moment, new inhabits of the dark fantastic realize they too are simultaneously a spectre and a monster.

At this juncture I will draw upon the self-description of the divine figure in the book of Exodus: "I will be what I will be" or "I will be what I create." In this manner, an infinitely variable divine entity becomes whatever form it chooses. My hunch is the divine has an inclination for the dark/mysterious. Very few examples of theological anthropology pay explicit attention to how Blackness embodies the divine or the human, outside of Black theology. This is nothing new. Black theologies would not exist if Black scholars did not take it upon themselves to explore the many facets of theological discourse from wide ranging vantage points of Black experiences. M. Shawn Copeland talks about Blackness and divine incarnation this way:

> "To reply, 'Black is beautiful!' disturbs the hegemony of a white, racially bias-induced horizon and shakes the foundations of its unethical deployment . . . [it] states a disregarded theological truth, nourishes and restores bruised interiority, prompts memory, encourages discovery and recovery, stimulates creativity and acknowledges and reverences the wholly Other…[as] our pledge to incarnate the triune love of God through acts of concrete compassion and solidarity in the here-and-now."[20]

Copeland is outlining the immediate effects of acknowledging divine Blackness by either one's own Black self or other Black people. Here, I will go a step further without any caveat. Black posthuman bodies are divine reality/God made flesh. This is an epistemological orientation. It differs from Copeland in that she is suggesting a psychic awareness preceding incarnation. In looking toward infinite variability I am suggesting that mere existence makes divine. If Black bodies are the result of infinite/divine variability (genetic, spatial, and temporal variability to name a few), then Black existence is perpetually divine, even into the mundane. I am arguing that being and remembering are different. I am also arguing there is no right way to be/embody God in God's infinite variability. Blackness, namely posthuman Blackness, moves in dark/mysterious recesses. Beyond the limits of human knowability where variability becomes infinitely more apparent. With infinite variability being a quality of the divine and Black people existing beyond humanity's limits, I then propose when Black posthuman subjects are witnessed the observers are seeing God disrupt/erupt into reality. The sudden appearance of embodied variability carries with it corresponding levels of uncertainty. The fear of the monster and spectre is also the fear of physical divine realit(ies).

It appears that a refusal to relinquish the reality set before white people through the avenue of imagination has placed significant pressure upon white supremacist realities. As a result, combinations of white supremacist realities attempting to form a composite are incapable of maintaining it. This reality is dying. The presidential debates of 2020 might have suggested American imperialism has reached the cultural capacity required to embody the religion of white supremacy; meaning this reality is already dead. The incapacity for seeing into the dark fantastic, is more cogently labelled as a refusal to see the ghosts/spectres and monsters as the divine figures they already are. It is also a reminder that the spectres and monsters persist, regardless of an acknowledgement of this kind of social/societal death: suggesting spectres and monsters are ultimately the future of subjectivity. So Black bodies, the monsters, the ghosts, exist as the divine. Being post- posthuman as the rupture of all humanistic iterations—including the posthuman. As this reality continues to die the once haunting aspects of Black embodiment will move from the periphery of dark unknowns through next world anti-humanistic biotechnological subjectivities.

Notes

1. Adam Frank, "If Dark Matter Can't Be Seen, What About Ghosts?" *NPR:* Opinion Science. September 16, 2016, at https://n.pr/3jkSCNn. [26 September 2020].
2. Philip Butler, *Black Transhuman Liberation Theology,* New York: Bloomsbury. 2019.
3. Philip Butler, "Making Enhancement Equitable: A Racial Analysis of the Term "Human animal" and the Inclusion of Black Bodies in human Enhancement." *Journal of Posthuman Studies*, *2*(1), 106-121.; Philip Butler, *The Black Posthuman Transformer: A Secularized Technorganic. Journal of Future Studies.* 24(2), 63-66.
4. Franz Fanon, *The Wretched of the Earth*. New York: Grove Press, 1963.
5. This lowercase usage of europe may frustrate some. I use it as a subversive measure against protonormative white supremacy and eurocentrism. Think of it as a posthuman measure to further decentre the eurocene.
6. Haifa S. Alfaisal, *Indigenous Epistemology and the Decolonisation of Postcolonialism. Studies in Social and Political Thought*, (2011) 19, 24-40.
7. David Woodruff Smith, "Phenomenology." Encyclopedia of Cognitive Science (2006); Bayne, Tim, and Michelle Montague, eds. *Cognitive Phenomenology*. New York: Oxford University Press on Demand, 2011.
8. Humberto R. Maturana, "Reality: The Search for Objectivity or the Quest for a Compelling Argument." *The Irish Journal of Psychology* 9,1 (1988), 25-82.
9. Arturo Escobar, *Designs for the Pluriverse: Radical Interdependence, Autonomy, and the Making of Worlds*, Duke University Press, 2018.
10. Michel Foucault, *The Order of Things: An Archaeology of the Human Sciences*. New York: Routledge, 2002.
11. Victor Anderson, *Beyond Ontological Blackness*, New York: Bloomsbury. 1995.
12. Patricia MacCormack, "The Ahuman", in Mads Rosendahl Thomsen and Jacob Wamberg (eds.), *The Bloomsburg Handbook of Posthumanism*. London: Bloomsbury Academic, 2020, 95-114; Jacob Wamberg, "Rising Negentropy, Evolutionary Reboots, and Gaia as Attractor: Toward a Map of Contemporaneous Posthumanist Positions", in Mads Rosendahl Thomsen and Jacob Wamberg (eds.), *The Bloomsburg Handbook of Posthumanism*. London: Bloomsbury Academic, 2020, 95-114.
13. Jasbir K. Puar, *The Right to Maim: Debility, Capacity, Disability*. Durham: Duke University Press, 2017; Achille Mbembe, *Necropolitics*, Durham: Duke University Press, 2019.
14. Friedrich Nietzsche, *Thus Spoke Zarathustra: A Book for Everyone and Nobody*. Oxford: Oxford University Press, 2008.
15. Harriet A. *Washington, Medical Apartheid: The Dark History of Medical Experimentation on Black Americans from Colonial Times to the Present*. New York: Doubleday Books, 2006.
16. Marquis Bey, "Between Blackness and Monstrosity: Gendered Blackness in the Cyborg Comics." In *Gender Forum: An Internet Journal of Gender Studies*, vol. 58, pp. 41-58, 2016.
17. Jaco W. Gericke, "Philosophical interpretations of Exodus 3: 14-a brief historical overview." *Journal for Semitics* 21/1 (2012), 125-136.
18. Aimé Césaire, "Discourse On Colonialism" *Editions Présence Africaine*, 1955.
19. Ebony Elizabeth Thomas, *Dark Fantastic,* New York: NYU Press, 2019.
20. M. Shawn Copeland, *Enfleshing Freedom: Body, Race, and Human Being*. Minneapolis, MN: Fortress Press. 18, 2010, 108-109.

The Posthuman Paradigm Shift and the Possibility of Catholic Religious Leisure

STEFAN LORENZ SORGNER

The posthuman paradigm shift implies that there is no longer a good reason for rejecting religions, especially those that emphasise love of neighbour. This does not mean either that any kind of religiosity must be plausible. The posthuman ontological weakening process leads to perspectivism, and an openness to the others, which means that any religion which demands violating or doing harm to others can no longer be regarded as plausible. This raises an enormous number of additional challenges. This paper critically deals with the possibility of religious leisure after the posthuman paradigm shift.

Leisure stands for the activity of reflecting upon the truth, our origin, and the nature of the world. Living a life of leisure used to be the core element of a fulfilled life in the Catholic natural law tradition. Without dedicating at least part of one's life to leisure, it was regarded as impossible to lead a good life. However, culturally a move has occurred which can be called the posthuman paradigm shift, which needs to be considered when reflecting on the possibility of leisure today. How can the posthuman paradigm shift be explained further?

The central move which can be identified with the posthuman paradigm shift is that from a categorically dualistic ontology towards a non-dualistic one. That is, it is not the case that the move can be described as an overcoming of dualism, as overcoming implies that a new duality gets created which would be a performative self-contradiction. It is more appropriate to refer to this movement as a twisting of humanistic dualities. The central features of a humanistic duality are that of a non-material rational mind and a material body. If the term overcoming was appropriate, then we would be left with a material body, but this is a non-plausible way of referring to the current events. We clearly have a rational mind, as we can speak, read and make logical inferences. All these capacities are mental ones. This is what we mean when we say that we have a mind. However, it remains an open question how the mind-body-relationship can be described further. When we talk about twisting the categorical ontological dualities which have been associated with humanism, then we do not get rid of the mind, but the meaning of the words "mind and body" get twisted. We still have a mind and a body, but neither exists independently of the other. They merely represent two aspects of the same entity, which no longer is a continuously existing unity, but a permanently changing something which is loosely connected in a contingent nodal point.

The concept of the twist corresponds to the German notion of *Verwindung*. *Verwindung* (twist) differs from *Überwindung* (overcoming) in so far as it is not a leaving behind of something. Overcoming leaves behind and separates itself categorically from the past, whereas a twist develops the past further in an inclusive manner. It is not the case that we get rid of the mind. Yet, we reinterpret the immaterial mind so that it becomes an entity which is the result of an evolutionary process. Hence, we do not overcome enlightenment anthropology, but it gets twisted. In the late fifteenth century, it was attested that "to wring", from which the word "twist" is derived, stands for the spinning of "two or more strands of yarn into thread".[1]

The immaterial mind and the material body get woven into a psychophysiological unity. What used to be the divine spark in us gets interpreted as a technological steering of an organism. We turn into cyborgs, that is, cybernetic organisms. The concept "cybernetic" comes from the Ancient Greek *kybernetes*, the helmsman. We are steered organisms. Being taught a language is a steering process, an upgrade of the organism, who we are. This ontological twist has enormous implications for incarnational theology, which needs to be rethought, as a categorically dualist ontology gets twisted into a psychophysiology.

Most critical posthumanists can subscribe to this description of our new self-understanding, as well as philosophically informed transhumanists. Yet, if this is the case, then we urgently must rethink notions such as knowledge and truth, too. In a world of permanent Heraclitean flux of everything in all respects, the correspondence theory of truth can no longer apply, as it demands the correspondence of a word and a thing in the world. If things are permanently in the process of change in all respects, but words are not, then a plausible type of correspondence cannot meaningfully be conceptualized. What we are left with are propositional judgements which can be understood as poetic metaphors at most, as Nietzsche correctly points out.

All philosophical judgements represent interpretations, whereby the term interpretation must not imply that the judgement must be false. It merely implies that the judgement can be false. Yet, in order to prove that the judgement is false, we would need a true judgement. However, so far, we have not yet established any true philosophical judgement. I am merely talking about philosophical judgements here, and not about judgements which represent tautologies, or judgements which are pragmatically true, i.e. judgements which usually work. If I board plane, I usually reach my destinations without any serious worries. If I order a coffee in an Italian bar, I usually get one. If I ask someone about the sum of 2 and 2, I am usually told that 4 is the proper reply. However, what the core of the world consists in is something about which we are uncertain. Only the final example represents a philosophical judgement.

The epistemological position which goes along with the posthuman paradigm shift is that of perspectivism,[2] which means that all philosophical judgements are interpretations, whereby an interpretation is a judgement which can, but which does not have to be false. To show that one's epistemological stance is self-contradictory, one would have to show that there is indeed a true judgement. As this has not been achieved so far, perspectivism remains a possible and plausible epistemology. This epistemological twist has an enormous number of implications; there is no longer a decisive reason for rejecting religions. However, if a religion wishes to embrace the implications of the posthuman paradigm shift, then the practical implications are significant, too.

Vattimo's Catholic weak philosophy takes this posthuman paradigm shift into consideration. He presents an option of embracing Catholicism which is in tune with this revised human self-understanding. A central term in his philosophical approach is that of the kenosis, which is "the condescension of God, the revocation of the 'natural' features of the deity", and which leads to the "dissolution of the sacral structure of Christian society" and thus to the "transition to an ethics of autonomy, to the secularity of the state, to a less rigid literalism in the interpretation of dogmas and rules".[3] Kenosis "leads to the overcoming of the originally violent nature of the sacred and of social life itself"[4] which implies that Christianity comes to itself more and more within the historical development. The sacred used to be violent, because it had an ultimate foundation, which guaranteed that necessary validity of ontological and ethical claims. Anyone who does not act in accordance with the demands of the traditional sacred laws fails, and needs to be punished, as the sacred laws are always universally valid in all parts of the world. However, such parts of a Catholic natural law tradition would not have been consistent with the posthuman paradigm shift. The sacred laws need interpretations, recommendations, and suggestions. What remains of Catholicism after the posthuman paradigm shift is the virtue of love. Love and do what you want, as long as you do not harm another person, your acts are justified, as this is what acting out of love means. One can assert that this idea is the basis of an incarnational theology. The Christian virtue of love is what remains from the preaching of Jesus Christ of the New Testament.

Analogous moves would have to occur to any religion, which embraces the posthuman paradigm shift. The ontological weakening process leads to perspectivism, which implies a distanced stance to all of one's most cherished insights, and an openness to the others. Any religion which demands violating or doing harm to other can no longer be regarded as plausible. This raises an enormous number of additional questions. What constitutes harm? What would a religion have to look like which avoids harming others? What remains from a religion once the traditional paradigms have been twisted? Here, we start raising a few critical questions, which demand a lot of further reflections. Which contemporary monotheistic religious practice is in tune with the posthuman paradigm shift?

The implications of the posthuman paradigm shift on the question of ethical implications of sacred laws demand further philosophical reflections, which has traditionally been referred to as leisure. Religious leisure has had a high importance among many Catholic theologians and was often identified with contemplating God. Catholic theologians like Josef Pieper or Pope emeritus Benedict XVI have presented some particularly insightful reflections on religious leisure.

In "*Leisure: The Basis of Culture*", Pieper stresses that leisure can be identified with "the stillness in the conversation of lovers, which is fed by their oneness… And as it is written in the Scriptures. God saw, when 'He rested from all the works that He had made' that everything was good, very good (Genesis 1:31), just so the leisure of man includes within itself a celebratory, approving, lingering gaze of the inner eye on the reality of creation."[5] It is the contemplation of the one, the unmoved mover in Aristotle, which comes up as gaze on the reality of creation, the origin and goal of all of us, as Benedict XVI points out in 2010, when he explains that leisure "requires a focus—the encounter with Him who is our origin and goal."[6] It is this understanding of leisure as contemplation, which is part of the Aristotelian natural law tradition of Catholicism. Aristotle clearly distinguishes between leisure and work, whereby work is an activity which we do primarily for the sake of money. Money is merely a means but not an end. According to Aristotle, playing makes up a part of working, too, as anyone who works also needs to relax from work, and this is what playing stands for. To play soccer, to have an Aperitivo with some friends or to watch a video are all different kinds of playing. These activities are widely interpreted as leisure activities. However, Aristotle refers to them differently. According to him, these make up part of work, as the meaning of all these activities is relaxation. Leisure, on the other hand, is an activity which makes us truly human. It is active philosophical reflection on what the world truly consists in, which is something all humans are puzzled by. Such an activity makes us quasi divine, as the origin of everything, the unmoved mover, permanently thinks about these issues, and by doing so we become quasi divine creatures. It is this tradition to which Josef Pieper or Pope emeritus Benedict XVI refer to. Hence, proper leisure is the contemplation of the unchanging truth which is founded in God alone.[7]

It is this essential element of leisure which demands further reflections, as the aspect of the unchanging truth is becoming implausible in the age of the posthuman paradigm shift. We have moved away from an understanding of an unchanging truth. This does not make it impossible to uphold a Catholic idea of leisure, but it renders it implausible to affirm a traditional understanding of the concept. Due to this development, the "originally violent nature of the sacred and of social life itself" got dissolved, as Vattimo points out correctly. Without there being an unchanging foundational and essentialist truth, there is no longer the possibility of reflecting on this entity, as no such unchanging entity is plausible anymore. This leads to the need to reconsider the possibility of leisure after the posthuman paradigm shift.

Furthermore, it needs to be reflected upon that leisure, nowadays, is not a central term within public or academic discourses. Work and dignity are much more central concepts. This also applies to the Catholic Church, as one can see when Pope Francis explicitly stresses that "Work is dignity".[8] All human beings are equal, because they all possess the divine spark, and in order to live a good life you need to work, Pope Francis stresses explicitly: "Without work, you can survive; but to live, you need work."

It is this self-understanding, which needs to be balanced out. Leisure ought to get the recognition it deserves. Ancient Greek aristocrats were ashamed of having to demonstrate to their peers that they, too, have to work. To reflect on our own condition in the world is what we are capable of and what we all are uncertain about. Leisure makes us truly human. Leisure is an activity being done for its own sake, not for the sake of money, as is the case with work. However, money is needed to survive. Whoever can dedicate herself to leisure also demonstrates a certain social rank by doing so: I am financially independent, I do not have to work. Leisure, understood in this manner, is an excellent way to moving away from a social climate primarily focussed on work. By considering this social aspect of leisure, reasons shine up why leisure as an intellectual, practical and sensual activity which is concerned with all fundamental philosophical issues ought to be given social relevance again.

At the same time, one aspect of leisure in this sense has become implausible with the posthuman paradigm shift. All perspectives being interpretations implies a certain doubt concerning an essentialist account of truth. Consequently, work as an activity which dedicated to the goal of making money, and leisure as activity which is dedicated to the understanding of truth in correspondence to the world is a categorically dualistic conceptualization, which has become implausible, too. A hermeneutic engagement with philosophical insights has become much more plausible. We read philosophical thoughts about the world, reflect upon these issues ourselves, and apply these insights to real life situations. Thereby, we experience the implications of our actions, which challenge our insights such that they can be revised and modified. Thereby, leisure turns into an activity which is not solely cognitive and reflective, but becomes more involved in a dynamic interaction between reflections and action, between *vita contemplativa* and *vita activa*. A contemporary account of leisure can be analysed as a twist of *vita contemplativa* and *vita activa*.

These insights have consequences for many different aspects of our lifeworld. School comes from the Ancient Greek word σχολή (*scholē*), which means leisure. It is a privilege to go to school. Schools need to be financed. School enables the young to dedicate themselves to useless activities. You learn to deal with numbers, words, and arts. Whenever, you learn something for working in a job, then you do vocational training. This should not the task of leisure or school in its original meaning. Hence, by reconsidering the meaning of leisure, we also need to reconsider how schools ought to be structured.

The same applies to the role of religious leisure. Here, the differences between Pope Francis, and Pope emeritus Benedict XVI are striking. While Pope Francis has pointed out that work (*labor*) is dignity, Pope emeritus Benedict XVI stressed that leisure (*otium*) "requires a focus—the encounter with Him who is our origin and goal." Jesus invites all: "Come to me, all who labour and are heavy laden, and I will give you rest." (Mt. 11:28). Pope Francis points to the relevance of the *vita activa*, while Pope emeritus Benedict XVI attributes more relevance to the *vita contemplativa*.

So what can religious leisure be like after the posthuman paradigm shift? On the one hand, it seems important to move away from work as a focus of dignity, and to reintegrate the relevance of leisure as an activity not immediately connected to making money. On the other hand, leisure can no longer be dedicated solely to contemplating the truth, as such an understanding of knowledge is no longer plausible. Do we have to choose between one of these two meanings of leisure? Why should it not be possible to affirm both meanings at the same time? Being forced to choose between the two understandings of leisure might merely be due to linguistic constraints, and the limitations of our thinking. In this case, the problem would be the language rather than the reflections just presented. Leisure is an important activity and it is one not primarily done for gaining money. Leisure is also a sensual, practical and intellectual engagement with philosophical issues whereby the contemplative, creative and engaging elements need to be twisted. Posthuman *scholē* includes *noiesis*, *poiesis* and praxis. Leisure is central for artists, politicians, and philosophers. There should not be differences between thinking acting and creating. All these processes form structural analogies.

Such a revised understanding of leisure has significant consequences for religious leisure. It can no longer be merely a contemplation of the truth, a return to the one, or a resting in God. All these elements remain important, but they must be balanced and integrated with *poiesis* and praxis. Religious leisure will continue to be an activity which is not concerned with money making. It will furthermore take into consideration the contingency of all insights and reflections, and the necessity of a continuous balance between *noeisis*, *poiesis*, and praxis. Catholic leisure can then mean to reflect upon the virtue of love, and its meaning in various situations, to practice love in one's *vita activa*, and to embody the virtue of love in one's artistic creations without being able to formulate explicitly, analytically and concretely what love stands for, means and implies. In a certain situation, it might be possible to possess an embodied realization that you have acted because of love. Then, you try to conceptualize what this love means conceptually, and it becomes impossible to do so. Based on the posthuman paradigm shift, a type of scepticism remains, which means that infallible certainty in God's existence cannot be realized. There is a need for contemplative reflection, and a reflective application of one's contemplations, whereby the contemplations are not targeted at unchanging propositional insights but merely on contingent nodal points or on as-good-as-they-get-answers which can represent helpful guidelines for the life world.

The most important insight of these reflections is that the posthuman ontological weakening process leads to perspectivism, and an openness to the others, which means that any religion which demands violating or doing harm to others can no longer be regarded as plausible, a key emphasis of incarnational theology. At the same time, there is no longer a good reason for rejecting religions. It is merely the case that the violence which used to be connected to the sacred needs to be abandoned. What remains is an openness towards other non-foundational perspectives toward which one needs to keep an openness, that is, an openness for discussions. If someone else is open for discussions, there is no need to exclude the other. Are there limits to what is legitimate in a discussion? Does it have to be a rational discourse? There is not one kind of rationality. There are different ways of consistent thinking. Does a certain linguistic violence exclude someone from the discursive field? This is not an easy question, and there is no final answer to it. This is what perspectivism implies. The need to question and requestion one's most cherished insights. Even if one has a contingent nodal point to which one holds on, there remains the need of reinterpreting the meaning of this insight, e.g. in the case of Vattimo's weak Catholic philosophy, leisure could mean to reconsider the implications of the virtue of love, and to apply them in the lifeworld. At the same time, there is a shift away from a primary focus on work as dignity. The Aristocratic primacy of leisure of Ancient Greek and Roman times will have to get reintegrated into our culture. This, however, does not mean a return to Ancient times, but it implies a twisted reintegration of leisure into our culture. Posthuman leisure is not an activity focussed on money making, but at the same time it is also not solely a contemplative activity. It is contemplation plus a contemplative *vita activa*, which can be interpreted as a type of mindfulness, a way to live out an incarnational theology. After the posthuman paradigm shift, leisure is an activity in which contemplative moments or *noiesis* get twisted with a mindful *vita activa*, which can consist in *poiesis* as well as praxis.

Notes

1. https://www.etymonline.com/word/twist [4 January 2020].
2. Stefan Lorenz Sorgner, "Philosophy as "Intellectual War of Values"" in Russell Blackford, Damien Broderick (eds), Philosophy's Future, The Problem of Philosophical Progress. Wiley, Blackwell, Hoboken, NY, 2017, 193-200.
3. Gianni Vattimo, Glauben – Philosophieren, Stuttgart, Reclam, 1997, 44-45.
4. Gianni Vattimo, Glauben – Philosophieren, Stuttgart, Reclam, 1997, 46-47.
5. Josef Pieper, Leisure, The Basis of Culture, St. Augustine's Press, South Bend, IN, 1998, 33.
6. Benedict XVI, Heart of the Christian Life, Thoughts on the Holy Mass, Ignatius Press, San Francisco, 2010.
7. Edmund Colledge and James Walsh (trans.), Guigo the Carthusian, The Ladder of Monks and Twelve Meditations, A Letter on the Contemplative Life. Reprinted, Cistercian Publications, Kalamazoo, MI, 1981.
8. https://www.agensir.it/chiesa/2017/07/13/pope-francis-work-is-dignity-the-words-of-the-pope-ahead-of-the-visit-to-cagliari/ [26 May 2020].

Part Two: Popular Culture and Posthumanism

How Church Online During the COVID-19 Pandemic Created Space for a Posthuman Worldview

HEIDI A. CAMPBELL

Posthumanism argues that humanity is in an evolving state of existence, and the human form is simply one of many stages in an evolutionary process driven by technology towards greater transcendence. In this article I argue that religion-technology and human-technology narratives closely reflect, and are connected to, dominant versions of posthumanism presented within popular media. By reflecting on these two sets of narrative frameworks, through the language used by religious groups to justify their embrace of technology during the COVID-19 pandemic I show how current discussions of religion-technology draw on broader discourses about the nature of humanity and technology in the created world.

While seen as a relatively new philosophical approach and worldview, it can be argued that the roots of Posthumanism connect with long established discussions about the relationship between religion and technology. Here, I suggest that contemporary digital technology can be seen through one of three religious narratives and one of three technological narratives. I argue that the ideals each set of narratives present are often evoked in popular discourse about technology in contemporary society. By connecting these two sets of narratives and their frameworks from my previous work, I seek to show how current discussions about technology that have emerged around religious groups' use of technology during the COVID-19 pandemic create a platform for the promotion of posthuman beliefs. I suggest that it is important for religious groups to be aware of the previous framings about the interrelationship of technology, humanity, and religion.

I Defining Posthumanism

Posthumanism is a term which has been understood in a variety of ways, from being a philosophical viewpoint to describing an emergent state of being or goal. In my work, I have defined posthumanism as "an ideology that foresees the overturning of a human-centred world, in order to make room for new technologically-enhanced forms of humanity."[1] This ideology asserts that humanity is in an evolving state of existence and the human form is simply one stage in a longer evolutionary process, which is driven by technological advancements. I see Posthumanism as an ideology that foresees the eventual overturning of a human-centred world, in order to make room for new technologically enhanced versions of humanity or being-ness. As such, this notion of the posthuman challenges traditional theological discussions of the nature of humanity. Thus, posthumanism presents a "unique worldview that sees humanity as evolving toward a new state of existence, where the human form is simply one stage in an evolutionary process driven by technological advancements."[2]

II Narratives about the Religion-Technology Relationship

There is a long tradition of comparing technology with spirit-like qualities. With the rise of computers and the Internet, the tendency to equate technological engagement with religious pursuits has been further strengthened. This equivocation positions technology in a unique position with religion, one that can create both a supportive and adversarial relationship between the two. For example, this was the case for the 2007 launch of the original iPhone, which became known online and in the press as the "Jesus Phone" in the time before its release.[3] Here, religious language and symbolism are used to create a story about the religion-technology relationship. I have three distinctive narratives that provide insights into different spiritual framings of the human relationship to technology. These include seeing technology as a) offering human redemption and godlike qualities, b) being seen itself as a divine or spiritual force, or c) offering humans a magical or religious experience.

Technology offers human redemption

The first narrative suggests humanity becomes godlike by embracing technology. Technology becomes identified with the idea of transcendence, whereby its use offers a gateway to salvation and redemption from the brokenness of the world and humanity's limitations. This presents technology as having an eschatological component, whereby it can restore humanity to its original state of perfection. This is echoed in David Noble's work on the history of the technological enterprise in which he calls the "religion of technology"[4] when human engagement with technology is seen as an attempt to regain some lost sense of divinity, meaning, and control over the world. This narrative frames technology as a form of salvation, possessing redemptive qualities, and having the potential to return humanity to some pure state in which it was divinely empowered. Yet, as Noble suggests, this is myth based on a false premise where humanity is deceived into thinking technology will provide lost powers that it never actually possessed.

Technology as a divine-spiritual force

In this narrative, it is technology itself that is seen as a divine or spiritual force. Here, digital technologies are framed as tools imbued with mythological and magical qualities. This dates to ancient times when created technologies presented humanity with godlike powers to create and communicate. Erik Davis calls this the myth of "techgnosis" where communication and digital technologies are magical forces offer us mystical godlike powers. Here, technology is often anthropomorphized, presented as a spiritual force empowering and guiding humanity into new possibilities and powers. As Davis states, "the fact that technology has catalyzed so much soul-searching suggests how mischievous and spritely a role it plays in the mutual unfolding of ourselves in the world."[5] This narrative suggests technology itself is a god to be worshipped.

Technology use offers humans a religious experience

This narrative claims that use of technology is based around a system of beliefs that suggests it can serve a religious role in society. Engagement with technology facilitates a form of implicit religion, where our practices and beliefs surrounding technology bear a strong resemblance to the role religion plays in society. Technology creates social structures, a sense of purpose and connection to something larger than the standard human existence. William Stahl described this as the myth of "technological mysticism" or "faith in the universal efficacy of technology."[6] The myth of technological mysticism frames technology as magical, and often fails to recognize the actual limitations of both technology and its human users. These narratives provide insights into different perspectives about relationship between religion and technology. These narratives also connect to, and in some case seem to echo another set of stories told by posthumanist about the relationship between humanity and technology.

III Posthuman Approaches to Technology in Human culture

Using religious symbolism and language is not exclusive to peoples of faith; in fact, much of the discourse about the potentials of posthumanism carries with it a strong religious quality.

Posthumanists often fall into one of three categories that demonstrate different understandings about humanity's connection to and engagement with technology. These positions are described by David Roden as: critical posthumanism, transhumanism, and speculative posthumanism.[7] While each of these positions understand the nature of human-technology relationship differently, they are all in agreement that a posthuman future is inevitable. As I will show later, these rhetorical strategies often mirror the arguments employed in other sectors of contemporary society to rationalize and promote engagement with technology in everyday life.

The technology-cultured frame: Online digital culture shaping humanity

One framework promoted within posthuman discourse emphasizes that technology innovation has created a culture that pushes us towards a future where the human form will eventually give way to a new technologically mediated existence. This narrative draws attention not only to the perceived human need to embrace technology but posits technological experimentation as the basis for understanding our evolving human world. Roden describes this as the category of "critical posthumanism," which dethrones the human subject as the core life form in our world.[8] Critical posthumanism privileges emerging technological forms.

I call this the "technology-cultured" frame because it presents technology as the superior partner in the human-technology relationship. Posthumanity is best explained through an embrace of emerging technologies whose values will shape our future. By prioritizing the role and influence of emerging technologies in society, the technology-cultured frame suggests understanding humanity within Internet culture is best done by embracing network technologies and the unique digital space and social structures they create. This frame highlights the way networked technologies have restructured our social realities and everyday lives. Describing digital technologies as aids that allow humans to transcend time-space boundaries becomes the basis for understanding the role technologies can and should play in our daily lives.

The enhanced-human frame: Humanity and the offline adapting to online technology

Another posthuman category that frames the evolution of humanity as one augmented by technology, asserts embracing a posthuman reality begins with evaluating our current human state and reconceiving it. Roden describe this position as "transhumanist' narratives."[9] Transhumanism emphasizes how technological enhancements can aid and advance human capabilities positively. Seen from this perspective, the goal is to become posthuman, which eliminates the ultimate human disease and weakness: death. In this approach a transhuman, is seen as one stage on the journey from being human to becoming post human. This suggests we are moving from the centrality of the traditional human form towards making room for a more highly evolved species enhanced through technological innovations. In summary, transhumanists believe in the moral right to extend life, enhance one's mental and physical capabilities, and embrace any technologies aiding these progressions.

I describe this as the "enhanced-human" frame, which emphasizes the opportunities offered by new technologies to extend human abilities. The enhanced-human frame loudly promotes embracing new technologies, based on the rationale that doing so for the betterment of humanity. Humans are called to embrace technology, because its unique affordances free them from the limits of the human condition. This frame insists we acknowledge the fact that the human state is already being enhanced by technology.

The human-technology hybrid frame: Merging humanity and technology in the online-offline

Roden's third category is what he calls "speculative posthumanism."[10] While speculative posthumanism opposes human-centred thinking about technology, it also understands any form of "technological singularity" achieved must be considered as a descendant of current humans. This position believes that technology will enhance human attributes in unforeseen directions. It is accepted that posthumans will "emerge via modified biological descent" and yet be seen as "recursive extensions of AI technologies."[11] This understanding sees the coming posthumanity clearly as a hybrid form, carrying characteristics of human predecessors, while existing in radically new technological form. Roden's says speculative posthumanist envision a future where a variety of unique posthuman forms will exist, as humanity is blurred out of existence through a reincarnation into new technological forms.

I describe this as the "human-technology hybrid" frame. This new technology-human hybrid however will not necessarily represent an equal integration of the two. It places emphasis on how various characteristics of humanity and technology can interrelate and inform one another, creating not just a new relationship, but potentially a new cultural existence. The "human-technology hybrid" frame creates a new state of in-betweenness, where memories or hints of humanity may linger on in a technologically transformed state of being.

IV Case Study: How church use and views of technology during the COVID-19 pandemic reveal a shift towards posthuman thinking

In 2020, the world faced a new disease which has impacted over 2.5 million Americans and 9.5 million people worldwide, resulting in almost 500,000 deaths with 25% of those coming from the United States alone. The COVID-19 global pandemic was more than just an international pandemic. In many respects, it raised important debates and issues about public perceptions of humanity, technology, and religion in contemporary society that speak to the issues noted above.

Several philosophers and technology thinkers have argued that developments and public responses related to the pandemic created an important moment, moving us closer towards the post-humanization of our culture. Mario Gabriele proclaimed in a popular tech blog online that "the Corona Virus has hastened the posthuman era."[12] By this, he meant that the health crisis brought on by the virus led to an economic crisis and social destabilization, which together spotlighted a cultural movement towards shifting understandings of the nature of humanity in our present day. Here, I would like to reflect briefly on Gabriele's argument about identity by considering how events related to religious institutions' negotiations with technology at this time suggest a shift in the understanding of human identity that aligns with certain posthuman positions discussed above.

Due to many countries shutting down their borders and banning public gatherings to combat the spread of the virus, hundreds of churches and places of worship were forced to close their doors and find alternative ways to conduct services. The common response during the pandemic in America was for Christian churches to opt for technology-based solutions. This meant quickly translating long established and embodied practices such as communal prayer, worship, and celebratory meals into mediated practices that could take place on digital platforms such as Facebook, YouTube, or Zoom.

A series of surveys that took place in spring of 2020 conducted by a collaboration of American church consultancy groups found most churches moved from offline to online-only services during the pandemic out of necessity. Facilitating religious worship online was a new experience for most of the pastors surveyed. Many of these pastors said they would have previously described themselves as technologically resistant to using digital technology in their church services. Yet social distancing policies and the centrality of the weekly event for most churches pushed them to reimagining church as a mediated experience.[13]

Since the mid-1990s, I have studied how religious communities responded and adapted to the then-new cultural phenomenon of the internet. Just as is seen with the introduction of any new media, the internet garnered a range of responses, from those who wildly praised this innovation and called for religious groups to utilize its potential to those who warned of the potential threats it posed to religious values and called for its rejection. The move towards distanced-mediated and disembodied worship marked an important moment for Christian churches and religious institutions, as previous criticism about the problematic values of technology were disregarded in lieu of full-on acceptance and praise for digital media to accomplish God's purposes. This position promotes the narrative that technology can offer humans a religious experience. Digital media serves a religious role in this context, enabling humans to not only connect with others across distances. It also brings them a lived experience of being part of the mystical idea of the body of Christ, which transcends time and space. Doing religion online thus begs an important question: "How much of religion really needs to be embodied?" When churches move from in-person communities to online ones, it begs the question: "Does religion need to be embodied at all to be authentic?" In a period where people are not allowed to gather, the very purpose and definition of religion comes into question.

This trend reflects what Gabriele describes as the transitional understanding of identity, being freed from time-space constraints of human embodiment. The forced moved of people to a physically distanced existence during the pandemic was accepted by many religious communities. Their embrace and adaptation to a new technology-driven reality suggests these religious groups, accepted at least for a time, that humanity can truly communicate, and the self can be mediated through technology. Such a position suggests an agreement, though maybe unwittingly, with Gabriele's understanding of how the pandemic reflected a new understanding of human identity. As he states,

> "The shift to a locked-in world has accelerated the acceptance of identity as distinct from physical body or place. We still want to communicate, socialize and play during this time, but have only a digital version to offer. Those constraints are forcing new expressions of selfhood."[14]

It allows us to transgress time-space boundaries of the natural world, to build relationships and find community beyond our human bodied form. The acceptance and embrace of religion or church online, thus reflects the beliefs in the "critical posthumanist" position that seeks to shift attention from claim that the human subject as the central life form. Critical posthumanism praises the embrace of a technologically mediated existence. Digital technology is the bridge that connects us not just to one another outside of the physical world, but to our posthuman future. As technology allows us to transgress time-space boundaries of the natural world, we find it is ourselves as well as relationships that we will be able to beyond our human bodied form.

This also exemplifies the "technology-cultured," where technology opens to us a new way of being that is superior to our limited human existence. Here, attention is given to emerging digital media to allow us to more fully experience the world. It prioritizes humans adapting to technology and to the superior potential it offers and encourages the embrace of network-based technologies that prophetically open for us a new social reality.

V Conclusion

This reflection on the justifications that churches have used during the pandemic to frame their motivations for moving quickly from offline to online worship have within them key assertions that link with posthuman argumentation about the human relationship to technology. By justifying their moves from embodied to a mediated, disembodied form of worship, they unwittingly promote a critical posthumanist positions. This is a perspective that encourages human assimilation with technology and privileges the technological enhancement over a mere physical existence. Church leaders' quick embrace of digital media as a tool to help the transcend the physical and social limitation placed upon them by the pandemic lockdown opens the door for them adopt a "technology-cultured" frame, where technology is seen as not simply a helpmate but a way to more fully realize humanity's potential. While most pastors likely would describe their embrace of the internet during this time as simply a utilitarian move, it must be recognized that their often-unquestioning embrace of technology mirrors the rationale used by critical posthumanists to encourage movement towards a new technologically enhanced human reality.

This move also demonstrates how technology is offering humans religious experience. The rushed move from offline to online church shows that contemporary religion sees and treats the weekly worship event as the central activity and expression of faith. It frames religion as event and experience based, and at this time only with the help of technology can the core of Christianity be realized. This position encourages religious groups to embrace technology in order to create a new religious culture that meets the spiritual needs of diverse populations both during and beyond the pandemic lockdowns. It suggests that church is most resilient when it embrace technologies as part of its religious practices. It promotes mediated over embodied religion as the more robust and versatile expression of lived religion in a network society. What it also shows is that religious advocacy of digital media is aligning with core arguments and using the same narratives about technology as used by different categories of posthumanists. This is not to say that all churches who use technology or church leaders who advocate for digital media integration to expand their work would embrace a posthuman worldview. But what it does reveal is the many general pro-technology arguments made by individuals in contemporary culture have within them kernels of claims on which a posthuman position can be built and advocated.

The purpose of this article is to showcase a range of key narratives about the relationship between religion-technology, and technology-religion that are often unknowingly employed by advocating for technology which can open space for promotion of a post-human future. I suggest that religious leaders and groups especially need to be aware of such discourse possibilities in order to offer a more nuanced response to technology that aligns more closely with their theological ideas of what it means to be human. Otherwise, their words and work may be co-opted for unintended ends and purpose that destabilize the position of humanity in our increasingly technologized world.

Notes

1. Heidi Campbell, "Posthuman" in Heidi Campbell/Heather Looy (eds.), *The Science and Religion Primer*. Grand Rapids: Baker Academic, 2009, here 177.
2. Campbell, "Posthuman," 2009, here 178.
3. Campbell & LaPastina, "How the I-Phone Became Divine, 2010.
4. David F. Noble, *The Religion of Technology: The Divinity of Man and the Spirit of Invention*, New York: Penguin, 1999.
5. Erik Davis, *Techgnosis*, New York: Harmony Books, 1998, here 335.
6. William Stahl, *God and the Chip: Religion and the Culture of Technology*. Waterloo, ON: Wilfred Laurier University Press, 1999, 13.
7. David Roden, *Posthuman Life: Philosophy at the Edge of the Human*. New York: Routledge, 2015.
8. Roden, *Posthuman Life*, 2015, Introduction.
9. Roden, *Posthuman Life*, 2015, Introduction.
10. Roden, *Posthuman Life*, 2015, Introduction.
11. Roden, *Posthuman Life*, 2015, here 22.
12. Mario Gabriele, "The Corona Virus has Hastened the Posthuman Era," TechCrunch.com, 01 June 2020, at https://www.google.com/amp/s/techcrunch.com/2020/06/01/the-coronavirus-has-hastened-the-post-human-era/amp/ [16 June 2020].
13. Andrew MacDonald, Ed Stetzer/, Todd Wilson (2020, April 14). "How church leaders are responding to the challenge of COVID-19," *COVID-19 Church Survey Summary Report: 2nd Round Survey*, 14 April 2020, at https://exponential.org/resource-ebooks/response-to-covid-19/ [16 June 2020].
14. Gabriele, "The Corona Virus Has Hastened," 2020.

Posthumanism in Popular Culture: Ongoing Challenges

ANDREA VICINI, S.J.

The increasing presence of posthumanism in contemporary culture can be traced in its multiple forms. After exemplifying this pervasive character and some of its manifestations, a few ethical concerns are highlighted by focusing on the posthuman moral agent, on the risk of escapism, and on the unquestioned trust in technology and its promises. Further, the critical assessment focuses on possible beneficial posthuman contributions, by empowering a selective questioning of humanism, as well as regrettable losses–notably human and social embodiment, which are central in the Christian experience shaped by the Incarnation.

With Michael Hauskeller and colleagues one can affirm that "[…] the idea of the posthuman and what it signifies, namely the surpassing of the human condition, is rapidly catching up and has now secured a well-established place in our cultural imagination."[1] Explicit advocates of posthumanism belong to a limited but growing group. Posthuman ideas and attitudes go beyond the philosophical, scientific, and political circles of posthumanism's devotees. Hence, the posthumanist presence in the cultural imaginary, and in its productions, calls us to briefly explore examples, point to some ethical concerns, and, finally, articulate a critical analysis that considers gains and losses.

I Engaging Posthumanism and Its Popular Presence

Posthumanism is inviting or, for some, even urging humankind to reconsider, revise, and modify what it means to be human and resolutely move toward a new understanding of our humanity. Hence, for posthumanism the human condition is in flux, and to fluctuate is considered both the standard and the goal. As the expression of its specific philosophical approach, posthumanism challenges any stable and constant framing of what it means to be human, whether in its descriptive or normative dimensions.

Openness to what humanity can and should become is posthumanism's dominant trait. Notable is the absence of criteria to define what could be limiting parameters regarding what is expected. Such open-ended dimension of posthumanism attracts and fascinates its proponents for the radical and plural novelty that it fosters and embraces. Humanity becomes like a series of multiple, maybe infinite possibilities of colours and nuances that an artist's palette makes possible. Posthumanism empowers an unbound variety of changes to what it means to be human. To anyone who feels entrapped in one's humanity, posthumanism proposes a way out, an escape, and an alternative.

Posthumanism depends on a perceived limitless technology, which intends to engineer life and the cosmos, in order to realize ecological, technological, and fantasized futures. Paradoxically, embracing posthumanism, seems to reinforce the exceptionalism of the Anthropocene by adding to it a new twist that further expands the technological, humanly made hubris within the cosmos aiming at what is perceived by its advocates as utopia and by its detractors as dystopia.

Interestingly, in the recent years, posthumanist advocates–whether in literature and other media or within philosophy–have embraced posthumanism as a new way of being in nature, with a concern for sustainability in the ongoing environmental crisis that humanity is experiencing. What seems to be absent, however, is the critical assessment of technology that it might not necessarily be the solution to ongoing environmental challenges–not even in the case of posthumans. Moreover, human-led technological misuses have significant responsibilities for contributing to cause the current environmental crisis and for not yet providing expected and anticipated solutions.

Focusing on cultural popular production, and considering different age groups, one notices diverse ways in which posthumanism engages one's imagination and addresses expectations, difficulties, and longings.

1.1 Literature
Posthuman stories aimed at children allow their readers to identify with animals, becoming them, exploring their belonging to nature in unexpected ways, usually precluded to humans. For Maija-Lisa Harju and Dawn Rouse, beyond nourishing the children's fantasy, these stories point to ways in which humanity should change–if it aspires to having a chance of surviving the environmental and technological changes that are at the horizon.[2] Hence, posthumanism is proposed as a way toward a reimagined, sustainable future.

In their book *Posthumanism in Young Adult Fiction: Finding Humanity in a Posthuman World*, editors Anita Tarr and Donna White gather twelve essays showing how posthumanism attracts adolescents, who are marked by the discovery of their changing bodies and new personal experiences of friendship and love, social isolation and difference, as well as cultural, political, and religious clashes.[3] As these stories indicate, posthumanism becomes a vector for an otherwise confined and constrained self-expression. As transitional objects in one's development, posthuman stories allow adolescents to portrait and narrate themselves in their journey through adolescence toward adulthood and help them to discover who they are and want to become.

Turning to adults, *The Cambridge Companion to Literature and the Posthuman* spans from literature to other media, including video games and movies. It gathers the contributions of a diverse group of scholars who trace the history of the posthuman by examining literary periods (from the medieval to the postmodern), explore literary modes (in science fiction, autobiography, comics and graphic novels, film, and e-literature), and engage themes (i.e., the nonhuman, bodies, objects, technologies, and futures).[4]

1.2 Comics and Video Games
Comics blurry the lines between text and image, as well as human and posthuman, by creating hybrids and challenging how humankind and the cosmos are represented. Fostering greater and active participation, video games and virtual worlds–like *Second Life*–frame digital landscapes that enable posthuman possibilities and utopias, including the modified and manipulated incorporation of religious concepts, longings, and images, as well as mythologies.[5]

1.3 Movies

A few movies could also be mentioned.[6] Technological singularity takes over in Stanley Kubrick's *2001: A Space Odyssey (1968)*. The computer with artificial intelligence HAL 9000 is emblematic of how humankind is stepping beyond its abilities to program and control what has been produced. Humanity is warned.

A few decades later, in 2009 James Cameron's *Avatar*, the protagonist Jake Sully is formed and changed by his own avatar and by what he experiences as a posthuman cyborg among the Na'vi race. Likely, the anticipated three forthcoming movies (2022–2025) of the *Avatar* series will continue and develop Cameron's view of the human and posthuman interactions with the Na'vi civilization.

Luc Besson's *Lucy* (2014) exploits the posthuman ability of using her whole brain, with its untapped potentialities, including uploading in computer networks and changing her physical appearance and her body's properties, at the point of becoming a swarm of nanoparticles.

In *Interstellar* (2014), for the director Christopher Nolan posthumanism means traveling in space through time and communicating with those who live in the past. Moreover, the only alternative to Earth's doomed destruction is technological singularity. Pursuing posthumanism requires trusting in human beings and their abilities to change themselves and make a future possible.

Ava, the robot protagonist of Alex Garland's *Ex Machina* (2015), mimics human emotions, by stressing how what we consider artificial and produced should become a part of the human, instead of the human becoming part of the technology. However, becoming autonomous, Ava makes us wonder whether human-made artificial intelligence will overcome human beings and masculinity.[7]

In Wally Pfister's *Transcendence* (2015), singularity is the technological uploading of the protagonist's brain in a supercomputer, marked by an increasing need for energy and an unlimited drive for power and control, which should be resisted.[8]

However, singularity is not exclusively technological. For Lee Toland Krieger, in his *The Age of Adaline* (2015), because of fortuitous physical events, Adaline remains youthful, fixed at her 29 years of age, for nearly eight decades. Hence, posthumanism is the unexpected possibility of an unspoiled and protracted very long youthful life.

Continuing to live in another body, kept in a lab, informs Tarsem Singh's *Self/Less* (2015), but the new body was a person and had a life before he was inhabited–it not simply an empty shell or a cyber-enhanced human like the main character Major (Scarlett Johansson) in Rupert Sander's *Ghost in a Shell* (2017). Hence, posthumanism is forced to deal with humanism, while one realizes its problematic trail, which required to perpetrate abuses and violence.

Finally, two 2018 movies – Claire Denis' *High Life* and Alex Garland's *Annihilation* – located on opposite realities, respectively in space and on Earth–articulate postmodern themes shaped by feminist critical approaches that decentre 'men.'

1.4 Philosophy

Despite their diversity, in these media cultural posthumanism expresses its philosophical sources by examining and questioning, in narrative ways, what it means to be human and what human nature entails in cultural and social contexts. Human subjectivity and embodiment are challenged, while striving to develop an understanding of the posthuman that is inspired by technological possibilities and imaginary opportunities.

For philosopher's Rosi Braidotti, posthumanism is not a threat to being human, but, on the contrary, the posthuman helps us in making sense of our flexible and multiple identities and of our place in the environment. It is the human, while embodying a disordered anthropocentrism and an anthropocentric understanding of progress and development, who betrayed what it means to be human and threatened sustainability on the planet. Within the humanities, as Braidotti indicates, the production of knowledge that is shaped by feminist, postcolonial, and race studies, together with gender analysis and environmental critique, informs a posthuman approach that not necessarily relies on individualism, but could foster opportunities for new social bonding and community building, while allowing to pursue personal and social empowerment as well as sustainability.[9] Hence, for Braidotti, posthumanism could avoid the criticism of its privileged focus on isolated individuals, who strive to achieve their own posthuman identity and nature. Finally, posthumanism allows to bypass opposed dualities, where the human stands in opposition to what is not-human – i.e., the whole environment.

II Ethical Considerations

While one wants to resist oversimplifying generalizations regarding the multifaceted aspects of posthumanism or a superficial dismissal of posthumanism's pervasive and diversified presence within popular culture, some ethical comments could be highlighted.

A first concern regards the predominant moral agent that is foreseen as interested in becoming posthuman: the self. Pace Braidotti's claims, which are philosophically bound, the communal dimension of being human, with its social and relational dimensions, seems to lose relevance. Culture is a collective product. However, posthumanism seems to envision and prefer an isolated subject whose agency is concerned about individual benefits to be gained and losses to be avoided. Identity does not occur in a vacuum, not even filled by technological surrogates. The other, and concrete others, contribute to shape one's identity for the better–when one's virtuous humanity is expressed by compassion, forgiveness, empathy, and justice–or for the worst, when anxieties and fears regarding those who are different lead to isolation and cause discrimination, marginalization, aggressivity, and violence.

Second, posthumanism seems to be the product of elites, of those who have the luxury of envisioning a posthuman future. As in other historic periods, what the elites propose does not remain within elitist circles, but overflows in society at large, even becoming popular to many. Compared to such a minority of people who are well off, most of humanity deals with pressing needs for survival–their own and of their loved ones. Posthumanism does not seem to be attentive to articulate a social analysis of means of production, consumption logics, work dynamics, and of all the multiple social and political determinants that influence people's lives. Inequities are not inevitable, but lack of concerns for them, aimed at their reduction and elimination, is troubling.

Third, one wonders whether posthumanism matches past escapist attitudes that responded to suffering and ordeals by pointing to future better times. Within Christianity, eternity was too often presented and preached not as a gratuitous gift out of love, but as the reward for the pain and struggles of one's earthly life, without providing sufficient criticism of the social causes of inequity and discrimination. The cross of the crucified people seemed inevitable. Only the eternal life could provide some post-factum and post-life restorative justice. Eventually, liberation theology helped to reframe these spiritualist and disembodied proposals by recentring Christianity on its commitment to promote justice here and now, without delay, as a more evangelically authentic response to the pressing needs of the least. Current magisterial teaching on social matters has embraced the preferential option for the poor as an essential, integral response to social injustice.

Fourth, the history of science, and of human progress, has stressed how it is necessary to examine critically any technological development and how they are socially pushed and received, as well as to identify those who propose them and what are their rationales. Technology has frequently promised to address human limitations and to overcome them. Authentic human and social progress, however, relies on technology in carefully discerned ways aiming at the pursuit of inclusive and shared human and social flourishing, which comprises environmental flourishing.

III Critical Assessment

If one engages posthumanism, by purifying it from ethically problematic tendencies, it is possible to identify elements that guide its critical assessment and that help in discerning its presence in culture, popular media, and social contexts. Like other cultural and social phenomena, posthumanism could empower the critical assessment of tendencies and dynamics that have characterized humanism and that hurt both human beings and the environment. What is needed are ways, strategies, and tools that could be beneficial for humankind and for the whole creation, with a particular attention given to those who are less well off and on the margins. Posthumanism could help to purify humanism from anything that is less human.

Christian theology, however, would stress that such inspiring role and responsibility should encompass appreciating our bodily nature, how human beings are embodied and social beings. Such appreciation neither implies ideological drives, which aim at divinizing both our bodies and human nature as such, nor any objectification of the body, which would consider human beings in dualistic ways, as body and soul.[10] Concretely, technological devices, even in the case of bodily implants that aim at restoring lost function (e.g., prostheses and cochlear implants) already contribute to expand how we experience being human. These technological incorporations are relatively easy cases because they mostly exemplify therapeutic interventions. However, more nuanced discernment is required when one considers technological or even genetic opportunities that aim at enhancing existing capabilities, while remembering that the separation between therapy and types of enhancement is blurry. Finally, the ways in which technology and bodies interact reaches its extreme in the proposed, still hypothetic uploading of our brains in supercomputers.

The scenario featuring the merging between our brain and digital networks appears to be ethically problematic on multiple accounts. First, it embraces a disembodied understanding of the self where the body does not count, is irrelevant, and can be discarded when time will come. Christian anthropology has human bodies in great esteem. Our body–with all its strengths, weaknesses, and limits–is essential to express and manifest who we are–our material, spiritual, and relational identity.

Second, it is reductive to replace our whole being–with its bodily dimension–with an exclusive attention given to our brain and its neuronal networks, disregarding the significant distinction between brain and mind. Human beings are a whole that is more than the sum of its parts or of an exclusive, privileged organ.

Third, human beings are always embedded in concrete contexts. These multiple contexts are not irrelevant distractions, like noise disturbances. Contexts contribute to determine and express who we are, what we do, and who we become. Whether one considers relational contexts–by focusing on their social, cultural, political, and religious dimensions–or whether one examines environmental aspects, in either case human beings understand themselves as contextually situated creatures, who exist and flourish in specific geographical places and determined historical times.

Finally, the mystery of the Incarnation allows to experience and believe how the divine, in Jesus, has chosen the limited human nature as a fallible condition and as a specific way in which what is sacred and what is secular become inseparable. Human beings can encounter the divine here and now, in their own bodily being as well as in others. The divine dwells in the human, not only in what is spiritual, in creation, or in

Scripture. The Incarnation neither divinize the human condition, nor stops inviting human beings to ask for the gift of conversion, becoming more authentically human, capable of care, compassion, love, mercy, prudence, and justice toward oneself, others, the whole creation, and God.

Notes

1. Michael Hauskeller, Thomas D. Philbeck and Curtis D. Carbonell, "Posthumanism in Film and Television," in Michael Hauskeller, Thomas D. Philbeck and Curtis D. Carbonell (eds.), *The Palgrave Handbook of Posthumanism in Film and Television*, London: Palgrave Macmillan, 2015, 1–7, here 1. Moreover, "the prefix 'post' does not come as an apocalyptic warning, but rather signals a new way of thinking, an encouragement to move beyond a humanist perspective and to abandon a social discourse and a worldview fundamentally centred on the human." Filippo Menga and Dominic Davies, "Apocalypse Yesterday: Posthumanism and Comics in the Anthropocene," *Environment and Planning E: Nature and Space* 3.3 (2020), 663–687, here 663. For examples, see Kim Toffoletti, *Cyborgs and Barbie Dolls: Feminism, Popular Culture and the Posthuman Body*, London: I. B. Tauris, 2007. See also Robert M. Geraci, "The Popular Appeal of Apocalyptic AI," *Zygon* 45.4 (2010), 1003–1020.

2. See Maija-Liisa Harju and Dawn Rouse, "'Keeping Some Wildness Always Alive': Posthumanism and the Animality of Children's Literature and Play," *Children's Literature in Education* 49.4 (2018), 447–466.

3. See Anita Tarr and Donna R. White (eds.), *Posthumanism in Young Adult Fiction: Finding Humanity in a Posthuman World*, Children's Literature Association Series, Jackson, MS: University Press of Mississippi, 2018.

4. See Bruce Clarke and Manuela Rossini (eds.), *The Cambridge Companion to Literature and the Posthuman, Cambridge Companions to Literature*, New York: Cambridge University Press, 2017. For a critical analysis regarding popular Christian views of the future, see Ronald Cole-Turner, "The Singularity and the Rapture: Transhumanist and Popular Christian Views of the Future," *Zygon* 47.4 (2012), 777–796, here 779–787. For more culturally situated examples, see Kavita Dalya (ed.), *Graphic Narratives About South Asia and South Asian America Aesthetics and Politics*, New York: Routledge, 2020; Denis Byrne, "Prospects for a Postsecular Heritage Practice: Convergences between Posthumanism and Popular Religious Practice in Asia," *Religions* 10.7 (2019), 10.3390/rel10070436; Enrica Maria Ferrara, ed. *Posthumanism in Italian Literature and Film: Boundaries and Identity, Italian and Italian American Studies*, Cham, Switzerland: Palgrave Macmillan, 2020.

5. On comics, see Katherine Kelp-Stebbins, "Hybrid Heroes and Graphic Posthumanity: Comics as a Media Technology for Critical Posthumanism," *Studies in Comics* 3.2 (2012), 331–348, here 336. See also Robert M. Geraci, "There and Back Again: Transhumanist Evangelism in Science Fiction and Popular Science," *Implicit Religion* 14.2 (2011), 141–172; Menga and Davies, "Apocalypse Yesterday." On virtual worlds, see "Second Life," at https://secondlife.com/. See also Robert M. Geraci, "Video Games and the Transhuman Inclination," Zygon 47.4 (2012), 735–756, here 739; Robert M. Geraci, *Apocalyptic AI:*

Visions of Heaven in Robotics, Artificial Intelligence, and Virtual Reality, New York: Oxford University Press, 2010, 72–105; Noreen Herzfeld, "Terminator or Super Mario: Human/Computer Hybrids, Actual and Virtual," *Dialog: A Journal of Theology* 44.4 (2005), 347–353, here 349–350.

6. For an extensive study, see Michael Hauskeller, Thomas Drew Philbeck, and Curtis D. Carbonell (eds.), *The Palgrave Handbook of Posthumanism in Film and Television*, New York: Palgrave Macmillan, 2015. For an ethnographic analysis regarding posthuman movies, see Claudio Pensieri, Massimiliano Andrea Vitali, Vittoradolfo Tambone, "Posthumanist's Values in Worldwide Movies," *Cuadernos de Bioética* 25.3 (2014), 397–412.

7. See Malcom Matthews, "Ex Machina and the Fate of Posthuman Masculinity: The Technical Death of Man," *Journal of Posthuman Studies-Philosophy Technology Media* 2.1 (2018), 86–105. On postmodern movies responding to the threats to masculinity, see Malcom Matthews, "Posthumanism and Miss Representation: Scarlett Johansson Is Getting under the Skin of Men," *Journal of Posthuman Studies-Philosophy Technology Media* 2.2 (2018), 166–183.

8. See Andrea Vicini and Agnes M. Brazal, "Longing for Transcendence: Cyborgs and Trans- and Posthumans," *Theological Studies* 76.1 (2015), 148–165, here 148–149, 157, 159. See also Heidi A. Campbell, "Problematizing the Human-Technology Relationship through Techno-Spiritual Myths Presented in the Machine, Transcendence and Her," *Journal of Religion & Film* 20.1 (2016), http://digitalcommons.unomaha.edu/jrf/vol20/iss1/21. [29 November, 2020].

9. Rosi Braidotti, *The Posthuman*, Cambridge, UK: Polity Press, 2013. See also Rosi Braidotti, *Posthuman Knowledge*, Medford, MA: Polity, 2019; Cecilia Åsberg and Rosi Braidotti (eds.), *A Feminist Companion to the Posthumanities*, Cham, Switzerland: Springer, 2018.

10. See James F. Keenan, "Roman Catholic Christianity–Embodiment and Relationality: Roman Catholic Concerns About Transhumanist Proposals," in Calvin R. Mercer and Derek F. Maher (eds.), *Transhumanism and the Body: The World Religions Speak*, New York: Palgrave Macmillan, 2014, 155–171.

Techno-Futures in Religious and Popular Art in the United States

SUSAN ABRAHAM

This essay examines popular portrayals of superheroes and their technological enhancements in US culture to explore how they subtly reinforce US White and masculinist Christian views of the perfect body, feeding into a larger rhetoric of White American nationalism. Such a thesis may seem to be in direct contradiction to contemporary theological analyses of posthumanism that argue that enhancement technologies violate the sacred uniqueness of the human body. In contrast, the success of a film like Black Panther demonstrates that technological enhancements can also work imaginatively, to mitigate the racism experienced by African Americans in the United States.

Popular culture in the United States is replete with images of technologically enhanced superhumans, who are often portrayed as "good" and "almost perfect" characters, yet who also must battle a dystopian world of impending doom and destruction. These superhumans, or superheroes, point to anxieties surrounding embodied life, particularly about bodily imperfections and imperfectly ordered gender and racial identities. On the one hand, a positive reception of enhancement technologies is situated in the very American ideal of "self-improvement" and the pursuit of happiness, supposedly available to all. On the other hand, enhancement technologies create even more anxiety because they are seen to disrupt the "natural" order of human bodies and their identities. This tension is explored in this essay through the representations of perfectability and technologically enhanced superheroes in religious art and Hollywood films because these aesthetic figurations depict the culture's deepest values about embodied life. These representations of perfection and enhanced humanity illustrate White Masculinist American assumptions about what it means to be human. In contrast, the genre of Afrofuturist posthumanism in Black literature and film embraces technological enhancement and the view of liberation it presents to African American people.

The pursuit of personal liberty and happiness is enshrined in the founding ideals of the American nation. Enhancement technologies are understood to be a way to accomplish both liberty and happiness for individuals, and as a fix for social problems, accomplished of course, by heroic figures who reinforce cultural ideals of the perfect American, who of course also deserve enhancements that will lead to more freedom and happiness. In popular culture the latter idea is fleshed out in the cult of superhero films, where heroes with enhanced selves "protect" Americans even as they may exhibit a generalized unease of their powers. In many ways, the ideal North American view of the ideal human self is one who is perfect, free, happy, and good. Gender roles play strongly into such idealization—men are virile and perfect protectors who are firm, yet kind, protecting family and nation when needed. Similarly, women are perfect, "pure," sacrificing and caring, especially about their families, neighbours and the nation. Enhancements are used in this context to increase personal happiness and perfectability, and in service of the collective recognized as the "great" nation.

Some contemporary theologians thinking about US Christian expressions of perfectability, assert that ancient Christian heresies about the body and its perfectability are reappearing in the quest for perfection and happiness. Richard Winter asserts that American Christians equate perfection with sinlessness. Since Jesus taught that his disciples could be "perfect as the Father in heaven," some Christians have thought that perfection is possible in this life. Two Christian historical strands of thought are relevant to his analysis. These strands, Gnosticism and Pelagianism, assert that perfection is a goal that is attainable in life, though in different ways. Gnosticism, as Winter points out, demands that Christians withdraw from the world, mortify the body and soar above the flesh. Pelagianism asserts that since Jesus spoke about perfection, it had to be an ideal that could be attained in one's life.[1]

Pope Francis in his letter *Placuit Deo*, speaks of the resurgence of these ancient heresies:

> A new form of Pelagianism is spreading in our days, one in which the individual, understood to be radically autonomous, presumes to save oneself, without recognizing that, at the deepest level of being, he or she derives from God and from others. According to this way of thinking, salvation depends on the strength of the individual or on purely human structures, which are incapable of welcoming the newness of the Spirit of God. On the other hand, a new form of Gnosticism puts forward a model of salvation that is merely interior, closed off in its own subjectivism. In this model, salvation consists in elevating oneself with the intellect beyond "the flesh of Jesus towards the mysteries of the unknown divinity." It thus presumes to liberate the human person from the body and from the material universe, in which traces of the provident hand of the Creator are no longer found, but only a reality deprived of meaning, foreign to the fundamental identity of the person, and easily manipulated by the interests of man.[2]

An obsession with bodily perfection leads to the neo-Pelagianism and neo-Gnosticism that the Pope warns us about. Of course, the arguments about neo-Pelagianism and neo-Gnosticism are also hijacked by US Christian fundamentalists who assert the primacy of Christianity in the United States. American Christianity is deeply driven by its desire for sinlessness and perfection. Here, representing sinlessness and perfection is instructive, revealing anxieties about ordinary embodied living.

Since there is only one example of the "sinless" human being in the Christian imagination, popular religious art attempts to depict perfection in specific ways. However, depictions of the Divine, especially in their idealized versions reveal that perfection is not available to all, even to all Christians. A particular example here is the image recognized world-wide as the Sallman "Head of Christ." This image which has been reproduced over a billion times around the world, has come to define what Christ looked like for many Christians. It is a thoroughly American image, reinforcing particular social and cultural values of masculinity and racial identity. Warner E. Sallman belonged to the US based Evangelical Covenant

Church and was a Chicago based commercial artist. David Morgan calls this image an example of "visualizing ideology."[3] Here, the image of Christ does not do the formal or liturgical work of the traditional icon, but "in accordance with the Protestant imperative of transforming daily life, Sallman's art has been most widely deployed in the everyday world—in the home, hospital, office, workplace, and purse—in hopes of influencing practical conduct by visualizing a properly Christian social order."[4] This image of Christ rather than capturing the mystery of the incarnation serves instead to reinforce existing social relations, specifically of race and gender. In other words, the image of a white Jesus with brown hair cascading down his shoulders as the image of human perfectability as a practice of representation, solidifies American race and gender hierarchies. A visual representation of the incarnation then becomes a tool of nation building and race consolidation.

Morgan's argument also asserts that unlike the dynamics of an icon, the Sallman image encourages a "mode of presence," rather than a mystical experience. The mode of presence emphasizes that the image is just that – an image. It avoids the Protestant suspicion of idolatry, but at the same time, strengthens the idea that Christ is immediately available to the viewer who then sees his humanity reflected in the image: an example of White privilege. The image does not make a claim about what Christ really looked like, but "imagines, in concert with a long visual tradition, what Christ looked like by revealing a particular character trait" as Morgan asserts. The trait is that of a gentle, approachable Christ, one that the viewer can easily trust. Morgan also reports that the image was not entirely positively received. A 1943 interview reveals that the Dean of the Moody Bible Institute, Reverend E. O. Sellers wanted a different image, where "Christ was forceful and masculine rather than weak and effeminate." In other words, the Sallman image of Christ, while signifying perfection, also reflected the anxiety of Christians in the United States: being kind and gentle like a kind and gentle Christ in the Sallman image demasculinized American male Christians. Christ for these Christians had to reflect American masculinist values about the male body.

Similarly, in another analysis, but now focusing on race, Edward J. Blum and Paul Harvey in *The Colour of Christ: The Son of God and the Saga of Race in America*, argue that late nineteenth century American

Christians worked hard to disavow any link between Jesus' Jewish ancestry and asserted instead that Jesus must have had a "Nordic" and Western European look to him. A critical idea in this study is that the colour and gender of Christ is intimately related to the broader narratives about America and White Supremacy: freedom, liberty, happiness and perfection belong first to those who can be most closely identified with Jesus. Debates about the colour of Jesus are unabated in US popular culture. Emily McFarlan, writing about the African American experiences with the Sallman image asserts that for many Americans, the Sallman image has become the only possible representation of Jesus.[5] For many African Americans, the Sallman image of Christ is formative and definitive. In recent days however, there has been a backlash to this image in the United States. McFarlan writes: "As protesters around the United States tear down statues of Confederate heroes and demand an accounting for the country's long legacy of racism, some in the church are asking whether the time has come to cancel what is called white Jesus—including Sallman's famed painting." Many Black activists are also calling for the elimination of white statues of Jesus, arguing that the blond, blue-eyed Jesus is both a cause and consequence of White supremacy.

If popular religious art projects American racial and masculinist fantasies of human perfectability, then popular film and comic books bolster these ideas even further. In fact, comic books as a genre articulate both the hopes of attaining human perfection through secular science and a fear of how science can interfere with the human, seen especially in the creation of superheroes like Superman. Superman (who presents as White with a perfectly honed masculine body) is chemically enhanced under earth's sun because he is also an alien, arriving on Earth from the planet Krypton. Published first in 1938, the story talks about a messianic figure with superhuman powers who aids and helps poor (almost exclusively White) Americans and the American nation. Because Superman is recognizably human, we can assert that he is an early popular cultural example of the post/human.

Dan Clanton Jr. states that the Superman stories have always contained religious resonances, though some see them as exclusively Jewish and others see them as exclusively Christian.[6] When Kal-El lands on earth, he is "found" by an elderly couple who bring him to an orphanage, though they later change their mind and adopt the child themselves, naming him "Clark." His adoptive mother, Mary Kent exhorts the foundling, "When the proper time comes, you must use [your powers] to assist humanity." As Clanton asserts, the Kents Christianize what could be perceived as a Jewish or even secular story: "the fact that Clark's adoptive mother is named Mary might be seen as reinforcing the larger theme that emerges with the introduction of ethics—namely, a parallel between Superman and the Christ of the New Testament."[7] Clark Kent is exhorted by Mary Kent to be "perfect."

But Kal-El's Jewish background and the parallelisms of the story to Judaism or Christianity disappear when the myth of Superman serves to reinforce American white supremacist nationalist myths. Superman is the epitome of perfection of masculinity and American morality, replicated in other superhero figures like Captain America and Superwoman. Within popular culture, Superman, and the rest of the Superheroes that followed are "posthuman" because their human powers are enhanced through technology. Scott Jeffery argues that these examples of superheroes in comic books and film are popular cultures imaginative constructions of "posthumanism" or "transhumanism."

For Jeffrey, comic books best depict the lures and dangers of posthumanism. The "fictive theory" of comic books is a reflection on the larger social context and a commentary on culture and social relations. The "man of steel" for example, reflects the machine age of industrial Western culture, but it is the body of the superhero that reflects the tensions of the age: "Superhero bodies are the results of industrial accidents, medical intervention, military super-soldier programs, and the techno-scientific machinations of corrupt corporations." Contemporary societies deeply impact the body; superhero comics thus are a "body genre." These body genres are then a form of cultural history, revealing a deep cultural obsession with body perfection.

In the Golden Age of superheroes, from 1938-late 1950s, the eugenicist view of the "New Man" implied that the perfect human body was a sign of the full flowering of White, Christian, and North American cultural power. After the 1950s, Jeffrey writes, the view began to change, following the negative view of eugenics and its importance for the German Nazi party. Superhero depictions in the following decades began to display ambivalences about perfect bodies and powers and began to display heightened anxiety and worry in the characters. In the sixties, Marvel characters, while still possessing superhero traits, also had very human flaws and were depicted as being prone to psychological illness, deep personal insecurities and as quarrelsome. In more proximate times, superheroes reflect the dystopian view of secular science that characterizes American evangelical Christian religiosity.

In a recent superhero depiction, a more subversive stance on technological enhancement is depicted, against the backdrop of the racialized context of American culture. In the blockbuster movie *Black Panther*, human beings that are technologically and chemically enhanced portray a vision of Black health and wellbeing, in contrast to earlier superhero films with almost exclusively White characters. Further, even as the film's characters display perfect bodies, they interrupt the connection between perfection and Whiteness. Contextually, it is important to note that the film is one in a series of anti-racist films that were released in 2018 and 2019 as a response to the disastrous presidency of Donald Trump. In this film, the posthuman is a challenge to what film critic Daniel Boscaljon terms "idolatrous whiteness."[8] As he points out, "whiteness," like "blackness" was manufactured to shore up the economic, cultural and military dominance of European colonialism that ultimately resulted in the creation of the United States. Whiteness now is a deadly influence on contemporary lives, especially in the United States, and in many parts of the world affected by American economic and cultural policies. Boscaljon writes: "Idolatrous whiteness is a major component of how the USA has systematically skewed the value of human life. All humans suffer in a racist world, but its consequences are more destructive for those who are not viewed as white. Historically, this has included Jewish, Irish, and Italian immigrants (who were not viewed as "white"), and this currently includes many Black, Latinx, Asian, Middle Eastern, Indigenous, and Indian persons."

Idolatrous Whiteness is not resisted by simplistically creating opposing heroes or repeating idolatrous forms of heroism. "Whiteness" is more than the colour of skin; it is a way of imagining gender, race and cultural superiority. As the example of the Sallman Christ proves, images and their narratives have the power to reinforce existing race and gender relations.

A Black "superman," would be a mere reversal, a form of multiracial whiteness, not the subversion of the idolatry of whiteness that anti-racist thought imagines. *Black Panther* performs a critique of Whiteness in such a complex way. As Ken Derry in an essay entitled "The Semi-Anti-Apocalypse of Black Panther" asserts, the film refuses to fully reproduce the standard apocalyptic and dystopian narrative structure of most superhero films while also rejecting the binary of Black vs. White. Unlike White superhero films, "the biblical end of times narratives, particularly their violent moral dualism: the forces of good, led by a lone messianic saviour, [that] destroy the forces of evil in a cataclysmic battle,"[9] are missing.

The film's central tension is built around the enmity Killmonger has for T'Challa, even though they are both Wakandan Africans. Killmonger, who grew up in Oakland, USA, (and his geographical place of origin has cultural relevance), is convinced that racism can only be countered by empowering and militarizing Black people.[10] T'Challa conversely, is of the opinion that compassionate openness to others will change hearts and minds. Critical here is how Black male identity is framed: T'Challa not only refuses to be defined by White Supremacy, but also is not a lone messianic saviour three women are critical to his success: his sister, his general and his significant other. Killmonger, who is also a descendant of Wakanda, is not a malign outsider, but someone who is the result of former decisions to isolate dissent within the Wakandan community. Since both are Black, there is no maudlin slide into the binary of Black vs. White. The film therefore does not construct difference monolithically. Both Killmonger and T'Challa are technologically and chemically enhanced, and each presents a view of the past, present and future in opposing ways, a difference of worldview. Eventually, T'Challa's gentle and kind ways (like a perfect Christ), wins against Killmonger's violence. T'Challa lives a "techno-incarnate" life for the sake of his people, effecting a rapprochement between technology and Black African American identity.

Black superhero comics, fiction and films belong to a genre termed "Afrofuturism." The term "Afrofuturism" was coined by Mark Dery, writing an introduction to three African American science fiction writers. His definition makes clear how Afrofuturism connects with posthumanism:

> Speculative fiction that treats African American themes and addresses African-American concerns in the context of twentieth-century technoculture, and more generally, African American signification that appropriates images of technology and a prosthetically enhanced future might, for want of a better term be called "Afrofuturism." The notion of Afrofuturism gives rise to a troubling antinomy: Can a community whose past has been deliberately rubbed out, and whose energies have subsequently been consumed by the search for legible traces of its history, imagine possible futures? Furthermore, isn't the unreal estate of the future already owned by the technocrats, futurologists, streamliners, and set designers—white to a man—who have engineered our collective fantasies?[11]

Yet, as other Black scholars also argue, Afrofuturism is about imagining a usable future for Black people using technology. Unlike a lot of pessimism about technology and its impact on human beings, Afrofuturist posthumanism embraces science and technology as pathways to a better future; a form of cultural resistance to the violence that is all pervasive in the lives of Black people. It imagines a vibrant utopia in specific dismissal of White expressions of posthumanist dystopia. Afrofuturistic Posthumanism in this view becomes the occasion to interrogate once again the idea of the human, who defines the human, and which human beings have rights. Technological and chemical enhancement become pathways to imagine a people saved from the violence of historical and continuing racism.

This essay has argued that cultural images of power, salvation and heroism are popular posthuman discussions, embedded in and reinforcing existing social relations. For Black people in the United States, the White images of Christ and Superheroes reinscribe US violent masculinism and racism. In Afrofuturistic posthumanism, we see an aesthetic intervention that overturns the literalist frames of US racism and by extension, debates on posthumanism. Here technological enhancement is seen as salvific; technological and chemical enhancement becomes the vehicle for African American thriving. When the Black human person has been sidelined in the cultural ways in which Christ and heroes are represented, a different order of incarnation must be summoned for the life of the community.

The possibility of a future creates a new consciousness for the enslaved consciousness of the African American. Technological enhancement offers a different way to think Black body and Black agency. Technological Posthumanism as Afrofuturism is relevant and meaningful precisely because American representations of human beings, heroes and the Divine, have never admitted the humanity and embodied salvific value of Black bodies. Afrofuturism thus is also a challenge to the debates on posthumanism that ignore the reality of racial social systems.

Notes

1. Richard Winter, *Perfecting Ourselves to Death: The Pursuit of Excellence and the Perils of Perfectionism*, Downer's Grove, IL: InterVarsity Press, 2005, 178-188.
2. http://www.vatican.va/roman_curia/congregations/cfaith/documents/rc_con_cfaith_doc_20180222_placuit-deo_en.html [15 May, 2020].
3. David Morgan, *Imaging Protestant Piety: The Icons of Warner Sallman, Religion and American Culture: A Journal of Interpretation*, Winter, 1993, Vol. 3. No 1, 29-47.
4. David Morgan, Imaging Protestant Piety, 34.
5. https://religionnews.com/2020/06/24/how-jesus-became-white-and-why-its-time-to-cancel-that/ [11 May 2020].
6. Dan W. Clanton Jr., "The Origins of Superman: Reimagining Religion in the Man of Steel," in Bruce D. Forbes and Jeffrey H. Mahan (eds.*), Religion and Popular Culture in America, Berkeley*, University of California, 2005, 33-50.
7. Clanton, *Origins of Superman*, 39.
8. Daniel Boscaljon, "Beyond Idolatrous Whiteness I: Resisting Racism," *Religious Studies Review*, Vol. 46, No. 2, June 2020, 265-280.
9. Ken Derry, "The Semi-Anti-Apocalypse of Black Panther", *Journal of Religion and Film*, Vol 22, Issue 1, April 2018, 1-8.
10. See https://www.oaklandca.gov/topics/oaklands-history-of-resistance-to-racism [11 May 2020].
11. Mark Dery, "Black to the Future: Interviews with Samiel R, Delany, Greg Tate and Tricia Rose," *The South Atlantic Quarterly*, Durham, NC: Duke University Press, 1993, 180.

Part Three: The Problems

Natality, Mortality, and Post/Humanity

JENNIFER JEANINE THWEATT

Theological engagements with the post/human often take transhumanism as the primary dialogue partner, leading to critiques of transhumanist visions of disembodied futures as "technognosticism." Taking the Incarnation as a theological reference point requires the Christian theologian to think through what it is about embodiment that is necessary, and what should endure as we contemplate and begin to construct what the post/human means.

I Introduction

It may be that the following takes on the character of self-musings rather than carefully constructed argument. I have elsewhere attempted careful and comprehensive argument, taking as one of my theses that the doctrine of Incarnation is newly relevant, especially relevant, in an age where human technological capacity and ambition makes new kinds of interventions on human embodiments an explicit and achievable goal, accompanied by rhetoric that often resounds with a faint but distinct echo of eschatological trumpet fanfare. In such a time, the Christian conviction that God intentionally "took on the human form and humbled himself and became obedient to death, even death on a cross" (Phil. 2:8), is intensely relevant, and graces the human body with a sacredness that forces a consideration of what precisely it is that we do, when we take up our tools and apply them to the body.

It is not self-evident what this observation implies, however. Does the Incarnation, as a concrete historical event, grace the human body as it existed in that moment, rendering all deviation from that concrete form undesirable, even sinful? Or, more abstractly, does the Incarnation simply give us reason to value human embodiment, or more abstractly still, material embodiment *per se*? If so, what does this mean for the task of living well together as humans made in the image of a God who took on our image in return?

In sketching these questions in this way, I have foreclosed on one theological possibility altogether, the possibility of disembodiment. This is not accidental. It is impossible to take the Incarnation as a theological reference point and tell a coherent story that ends with the conclusion that bodies are dispensable, inconsequential, unnecessary or undesirable. As the Christian theological dialogue with transhumanism and post/humanism has progressed over the last decade, perhaps the one firm theological consensus to have emerged is this: an emphatic 'Nein!' to the secular-eschatological visions of human futures that imagine a disembodied existence as a desirable one.

II The 'false problem' of disembodiment

As I argue elsewhere, which version of the post/human imagination theologians engage with is a significant preliminary decision that definitively shapes the content of the dialogue. Theologians engaging with the post/human who begin with Donna Haraway's "Cyborg Manifesto" as the dialogue partner enter into a different conversation than those who being with humanityplus.org's "Transhumanist FAQ." The issue of embodiment, in particular, is at stake in a particular way in these two different conversations.

As Jeffrey Pugh observes, many theologians in dialogue with transhumanism have characterized it as a kind of "technognosticism," in that it shares with ancient Gnosticism an explicit desire to escape the limitations of the material body.[1] This is at is most explicit in transhumanist descriptions of the "upload scenario," a thought experiment in which an individual's consciousness is scanned, replicated and reinstantiated in a substrate other than the original body (usually presumed to be a virtual environment). Setting aside the obvious and intriguing questions of personhood, identity, and continuity of the first-person experiential point of view—all worthwhile questions philosophically—and granting for the moment that such a scenario is plausible enough to be worth entertaining, the point of such a scenario seems undeniably to be escape from a biological embodiment that limits the consciousness.

Alternatively, to start the conversation with Haraway's cyborg is to start a post/human theological dialogue about the body. As I have argued elsewhere, the cyborg is defined by its specific embodied hybridity. For Haraway, the cyborg's usefulness as a figure lay in its ability to challenge the "dualisms of mind and body, animal and machine, idealism and materialism in the social practices, symbolic formulations, and physical artifacts associated with 'high technology' and scientific culture."[2] These dualisms existed not only in the political, philosophical and theological discourses of Western culture dominated by patriarchal assumptions and structures, but within the second-wave feminist response to those discourses and structures as well, in the valorization of the natural, the feminine, the maternal, as opposed to the technological, the masculine, the patriarchal. The cyborg is not a flight from the body, but a body which defies dualistic categorization. That's the point of it.

The trajectory of this conversation moves us, not away from the body, but closer to it, to questions of specificity, hybridity and multiplicity. It moves to connections with queer theology, about the multiplicity of human embodiments with regard to sex and gender; it moves to connections with disability theology, about the multiplicity of human embodiments with regard to physical form and ability and the definition of norms; it moves to connections with postcolonial theology, about the multiplicity and diversity and hybridity of human embodiments and identities with regard to social, cultural, and political categories such as race and ethnicity and citizenship.[3]

So I take as my starting point an admonition voiced by Donna Haraway: "These ontologically confusing bodies, and the practices that produce specific embodiment, are what we have to address, not the false problem of *dis*embodiment."[4] Yet for the most part, theological engagement with the post/human have taken transhumanism as the dialogue partner. I want to point out that if this is the only post/human vision with which we engage, we are missing out on the real and vital dialogue around "ontologically confusing *bodies*, and the practices that produce specific embodiment," which not only engages imaginative visions of desirable futures but concrete matters of immediate importance, theologically and ethically, regarding the kinds of interventions on the body and the kinds of reasons for these interventions that we deem acceptable (or at least, accept, without having realized and seized the preliminary moment of ethical consideration thereof). It is here that we should, I propose, spend most of our time as theologians; having claimed that human embodiments are a divinely given and graced good, can we identify what is good about it, and identify how this directs our actions in relation to ourselves, others and to God?

In echoing Haraway's claim that technological visions of future disembodiment are a "false problem," however, I do not mean to suggest a kind of facile dismissal on the grounds of a God-of-the-gaps objection of apparent impossibility. Perhaps such visions are impossible; to be honest, I think that they are, on the grounds of being badly mistaken about what it means to be human—an ontological rather than technical impossibility. Yet even so, we ought, as theologians, consider these visions for what they can teach us of human imagination and desire, regardless of questions of plausibility. For this reason, transhumanist dreams of escaping the body are instructive.

What, then, do these disincarnate dreams tell us about those who dream these things? Elaine Graham has suggested that the transhumanist vision of an uploaded consciousness demonstrates not "so much a love of life, as, paradoxically, a pathological fear of death, vulnerability and finitude."[5] Aspirations toward a digitalized post-biological humanity, she writes, often reflect a disdain for the mortality of the flesh; technology is the mechanism of protecting the self against fears of vulnerability. This reading of transhumanism suggests that the ultimate motivation is not actually immortality *per se*—in digital form or otherwise—but invulnerability.

III Theological Investigations of Post/humanism

If, then, we as Christian theologians insist upon embodiment, and with it, finitude and vulnerability, why? What account can we give, theologically, that makes a compelling case for finitude, vulnerability and death? How do we do this without valourizing suffering as itself redemptive, or appealing to notions of natural limit which no longer maintain any plausibility given what we know about the malleability of human nature? To answer this question, I want to briefly switch gears, and appeal to the work of Karl Rahner.

In 1965, Karl Rahner directly addressed the question of what, if anything, a theologian can or should say about what he called "man's self-manipulation," what we, decades later, are referring to as the post/human.[6] Published in English as "The Experiment with Man: Theological observations on man's self-manipulation," this essay avoids a casuistic ethics about specific technologies and attempts instead to sketch a theological stance toward questions of human enhancement and post/human possibility grounded in Rahner's concept of the relation of the human to God. What follows is a close reading of an essay that, although not directly referenced in any previous work of mine, has informed and influenced my theological stance on these questions.

Rahner's essay offers, as a starting point, an argument for "Christian cool-headedness" in the face of humanity's future (210). This is the proper Christian attitude toward the future, even the possibility of something like a post/human future, because humans have always been, in Rahner's term, "operable:"

Man has purposely drunk wine to combat his melancholy; consciously used coffee as a stimulant; undertaken primitive attempts at human breeding; endeavoured to change his bodily form by means of various techniques, beginning with shaving; conceived the practice of education in terms of artificially superimposing knowledge instead of cultivating insight…Man plans his own self; in much he is still groping his way, seeking the goals of his self-manipulation and only perceiving the possibility of realizing them in the remote distance (207).

These observations align Rahner with posthuman thinkers who have argued along these same lines that "we have always been cyborgs."[7] In this sense, nothing fundamentally new is happening, and certainly nothing worth becoming alarmed about.

If there is anything new here, Rahner suggests that it is that we are discovering that we are 'operable,' and able to be more systematic and intentional in the ways that we operate. This makes enough of a difference, however, that Rahner describes this as a "radically new period," and suggests that this new form of self-manipulation can be distinguished from previous "preliminary instances" in the following ways: it is multi-dimensional; it is focused on the human being as an empirical (not spiritual or transcendental) subject; it is systematic and long-term; it concerns the human being as a whole; it concerns humanity as a whole rather than individual persons. Rahner writes,

It is not concerned with this or that man but with man, with mankind; it does not wish to conjure up a utopia of supermen within a profanised eschatology, but coolly to sketch, design and calculate a new, different man and then to produce him technologically in accordance with this plan (207-8).

Rahner does not imagine that this is a coordinated movement, though I don't suppose that the emergence of transhumanism in the late 80's and early 90's would have surprised him. He describes the production of this new, different human being as the convergences of several different interests in multiple fields, which eventually may become coordinated politically.

So far this factory for the new man does not exist. But it is as though buildings are being constructed simultaneously all over a great site, and one has the impression that these separate constructions will eventually grow into a single complex—into a hominised world. This is the one immense factory where 'operable' man dwells in order to invent himself (209).

Even if, however, there is something in this new era which is distinctive about humanity's ability to self-manipulate along these lines, "Christian cool-headedness" remains the appropriate theological stance, as opposed to either reactionary opposition or uncritical endorsement. This is true even if "possibilities are becoming apparent…which are immoral and unworthy and which may indicate a 'Fall,'" and even while Christians must "have the courage to oppose with utter resoluteness those kinds of self-manipulation which are the most recent forms of barbarity, slavery, the totalitarian annihilation of personality and formation of a monochrome society" (211). Even so, the reality that "man is fundamentally 'operable,' and legitimately so," means that "the Christian has no reason to enter this future as a hell on Earth nor as an earthly kingdom of God. Jubilation or lamentation would run counter to the Christian's cool-headedness" (212).

Moreover, Rahner connects the fundamentally 'operable' nature of human beings, and the capacity for self-manipulation, to the "self-determination as the nature and task of man's freedom as understood by Christianity" (212). Intriguingly, Rahner sees spiritual and transcendental means of self-manipulation as part of the historical preliminary to the "radical new age" of self-manipulation in the empirical sense. From this perspective, then, self-manipulation of the empirical self is an extension of the self-manipulation of the spiritual or transcendental self, which Rahner views as definitive for the human being. (213) This orientation shifts the "Christian cool-headedness" Rahner prescribes from a completely neutral viewpoint into a cautiously positive one.

It is this, I think, that leads Ron Cole-Turner to lean on Rahner's work as the springboard for his own argument that "transhumanism is a Christian concept," a claim often made by proponents of Christian Transhumanism.[8] Cole-Turner writes, "As Rahner puts it, 'the transcendence of man makes it clear that it would be wrong to define him, to delimit and put bounds to its possibilities.'"[9] This, I think, pushes an interpretation Rahner too far, away from "cool-headedness" into a kind of mistaken jubilation.

Moreover, to frame things in this way obscures the differences between secular transhumanist visions of possible futures, and Christian visions of what Rahner calls the "absolute future." Elsewhere, Cole-Turner takes this into account, acknowledging that within Rahner's thought there is a distinction between the "next things," the intramundane future, and the "last things," the "absolute future," which is the union of all creation with God: "The difference between these futures is not based on their coming at a different place in the temporal order of the sequence of events…The difference is ontological and theological, not sequential or historical."[10] While Rahner argues that there are no non-arbitrary limits to what may be done in terms of human self-manipulation on the empirical self, as an extension of the larger, essentially human project of self-transcendence, this takes place within the horizon of the absolute future, which is ultimately the mystery of God.

As Rahner himself recognizes, "It is very difficult to define the highly differentiated relationship between anticipating the absolute, eschatologically occurring future in faith and theological hope on the one hand, and anticipating the intramundane future by means of planning and active self-manipulation on the other hand" (219). Rahner's solution to this difficulty is to insist on locating the human activity of self-manipulation as a new extension of an essentially human activity, within an intramundane future which is itself taken up into the absolute future determined by

God—which, Rahner says, both critiques and unmasks this activity as non-absolute, and confirms it as appropriate (219).

Maintaining the balance of emphasis on both the positive and negatives poles of this nuanced position is a delicate matter. On the one hand, shaping the future is "a Christian task," one which Rahner wishes more Christians were actively involved in: "One ought to complain that… Christians contribute so little courage and creative imagination to an ideology of the future for this self-manipulation, but are generally content to provide conservative admonitions and obstructions" (220, 224). On the other hand, in sharp contrast to the transhumanist ambitions of at least theoretically endless life extension, Rahner identifies quite specifically the place where empirical self-manipulation meets its limit if it is to remain an extension of the essential human task of self-transcendence: death, he writes, is the permanent door to the absolute future (221).

What Rahner means by this is not a defence of current physical limitations, or a defence of suffering as itself redemptive. Rather, it is that death is the marker of an inevitable finitude of the human subject, regardless of what forms of self-manipulation are or are not attempted. In Rahner's view, it seems to be a given that regardless of what technical finesse humanity may develop, our manipulations of self and environment take place within a universe that will never be fully under human control. Therefore, "every plan, every pre-set and pre-calculated system gives rise to new elements which were not planned and not scheduled, because it is constructed of pre-existing elements which can never be adequately penetrated and categorized" (222). Human beings are able to recognize this, Rahner suggests; the fundamental question, regardless of what forms of self-manipulation take place within the human and post/human future, is not, then, how to delay or avoid or defeat this death, but "whether this unfathomable thing which surrounds him is the void of absolute absurdity or the infinitude of the mystery of love, the absolute future which is reached through death, so that only by accepting it and can really discover and 'invent' himself" (222-3). Death, then, is not defeat, because a "win" is not actually possible; it is, rather, the exit from the intramundane into the absolute future.

This death is not only the zero hour though which the individual must pass on his way to the absolute future, but also the zero hour for mankind as a whole...No stars need fall from heaven; it can be the end as a result of genocide; it can be a social end (as a result of atom bombs, for instance); a physical end in a world catastrophe; it could be (who can know for sure?—the Christian must take even absurdity into account) that mankind might actually regress biologically to the level of technically intelligent and self-domesticated aboriginal herd or an insect-state without the pain of transcendence, history and the dialogue with god. I.e. it might extinguish itself by collective suicide, even if it were to continue to exist at the biological level. A Christian theology of history basically need not take fright at such an idea in itself...for it knows that the history of men always ultimately arrives at God...or else it simply ceases to be the history of spiritual persons at all (223).

For Rahner, the concrete form of human embodiment is not the issue; self-manipulation of what he calls the empirical self is not forbidden, and is, in his view, part of what human beings have always done and should be doing as an expression of transcendence. This leads to a direct rebuttal of any theologizing that depends upon concepts of a divinely given, static essential "nature" that somehow must not be tinkered with. But it is possible, Rahner thinks, for self-manipulation to go awry. This may happen in two ways: if humanity mistakenly assumes that any mistakes can simply be corrected, erased or reversed through subsequent manipulation rather than understanding that human action takes place within a unidirectional history, and that self-manipulation carries irreversible consequences; secondly, if humanity fails to undertake self-manipulation as an expression of "the concrete, active expression of the love of one's fellows, making possible the 'openness' to God's absolute future, even if it cannot itself bring about this absolute future" (221). If, as Rahner states here, the motivation of proper self-manipulation is to continue "to make possible the 'openness' to God's absolute future" for humanity and post/humanity, two things, I suggest, are implied: first, and most obviously, that death as the "permanent door to the absolute future" is not an aspect of the empirical self that can be manipulated; and second, that forms of self-manipulation that quest after invulnerability are a theological and ethical mistake.

IV Incarnation as the divine embrace of vulnerability

But thus far I have said nothing concerning the Incarnation, for the simple reason that the Incarnation is not a theological locus that shows up directly in Rahner's "The Experiment with Man." I want to suggest that one of the aspects of the Incarnation most pertinent to post/human discussions is the divine embrace of vulnerability. To explore this, I rely on Elizabeth O'Donnell Gandolfo's exploration of natality and vulnerability in the doctrine of Incarnation.

As Gandolfo observes, theological reflection on the person and saving work of Christ is often primarily concerned with the adult man Jesus, his ministry, his death, and the salvation that his life, death and resurrection offer to sinful humanity; but, "the liberating good news of divine incarnation does not begin with Jesus' public ministry as an adult. Rather, it begins with a socially high-risk pregnancy; with a humble, messy and painful birth; and with the natal body of a squalling, dependent and vulnerable infant." Focusing too exclusively on "the divinity present in the agency of an adult male fails to drive home the utter contingency and inevitability of vulnerability faced by divine love in the Incarnation;" it allows us to minimize, to imagine that nothing much was risked, and perhaps nothing much was suffered.[11]

But to begin with the vulnerable infant Jesus, and to recall the dependency of the human infant on caregivers to supply every need, emphasizes that vulnerability is a universal dimension of human life. Maturing into adults allows an illusion of autonomy, but at no point is the human being self-sufficient; we remain dependent on externalities to supply our needs, both physically and socially. The nature of this dependency on externalities means that human beings are "thus constantly and from the very beginning faced with the threat of harm, of pain, of suffering, and ultimately, of death. Natality and mortality cannot be separated."[12]

The answer to such vulnerability is not to seek means of avoiding it, but to seek ways to answer it: to supply the needs of those around us. As Gandolfo observes, human beings seek to escape this through a flight to invulnerability, often through violence—to ourselves or to others.[13] In this context, we can also add, through our technological imaginations. But this ignores the obvious alternative: the answer to vulnerability is care.

There is an intriguing overlap in the way that Grace Jantzen's work on natality informs both Gandolfo's exploration of the Incarnation, and Elaine Graham's exploration of expressions of transcendence in the post/human. Gandolfo writes, "In [Jantzen's] view, it is natality that actually forms the unacknowledged foundation of the Western obsession with death and the consequent drive for mastery," an insight that informs Graham's read of transhumanist aspirations of digitized immortality as an expression, not of expansive love of life, but pathological fear of death and vulnerability.[14] And here. As well, Rahner's description of death as the "permanent door to the absolute future," becomes less abstractly theoretical.

Whatever it is that we do as we build our post/human futures, and whatever cyborg embodiments we craft for ourselves, if our aim is a future in which we are invulnerable, we miss the mark. In the Incarnation, God becomes embraces vulnerability in order to demonstrate, that whatever form our humanity takes, the answer to our vulnerable being is, in Rahner's phrase, that we ultimately belong to "the mystery of love."

Notes

1. Jeffrey Pugh, "The Disappcaring Human: Gnostic Dreams in a Transhumanist World," Religions 8, 81, doi:10.3390/rel8050081.
2. Donna Haraway, "A Cyborg Manifesto: Science, Technology and Socialist-Feminism in the Late Twentieth Century," in Simians, Cyborgs and Women: The Reinvention of Nature, New York: Routledge, 1991, 149-81, here 154.
3. For further initial explorations of these connections, see Jeanine Thweatt, Cyborg Selves: A Theological Anthropology of the Posthuman, Burlington, VT: Ashgate, 2012.
4. Donna Haraway, "Fetus: The Virtual Speculum in the New World Order," in Modest_Witness@Second_Millennium.FemaleMan©_Meets_OncoMouse™:Feminism and Technoscience, New York: Routledge, 1997, 173-212, here 186.
5. Elaine Graham, Representations of the Post/human: Monsters, Aliens, and Others in Popular Culture, New Brunswick, NJ: Rutgers University Press, 2002, 230.
6. Karl Rahner, "The Experiment with Man: Theological observations on man's self-manipulation," in Theological Investigations vol. IX: Writings of 1965-1967, translated by Graham Harrison, New York: Herder and Herder, 1972, 205-224. Subsequent references to this text are parenthetical. Note: In direct quotes, the author has retained the translation's use of "man," "mankind," and the masculine pronouns to refer to humanity in the interest of historical accuracy, though inclusive language is used as appropriate when paraphrasing.
7. Haraway, for example, and N. Katherine Hayles, How We Became Poshuman: Virtual Bodies in Cybernetics, Literature and Informatics, Chicago: University of Chicago Press, 1999.
8. Cole-Turner, Ron. "Going Beyond the Human: Christians and Other Transhumanists," Dialog: A Journal of Theology 54.1 (2015): 20-26.

9. Cole-Turner, "Going Beyond the Human;" Rahner, Karl. "On the Theology of the Incarnation," trans. by Kevin Smith, Theological Investigations, vol. 4 (Baltimore: Helicon Press, 1966), 107.
10. Cole-Turner, Ron. "Eschatology and the Technologies of Human Enhancement," Interpretation: A Journal of Bible and Theology 70.1 (2016): 27.
11. Elizabeth O'Donnell Gandolfo, "A Truly Human Incarnation: Recovering a Place for Nativity in Contemporary Christology," Theology Today 70 (2013): 384.
12. Gandolfo, "Nativity," 386.
13. Gandolfo, "Nativity," 393.
14. Gandolfo, "Nativity," 385.

Eucharistic Cyborgs and the Real (Carnal) Presence of Christ

JAY EMERSON JOHNSON

The restrictions placed on physical gatherings by the Covid-19 pandemic have raised questions in some religious communities about the "validity" of online rituals and sacramental acts. These restrictions have likewise surfaced a deep hunger for the Eucharist in nearly every Christian community. Exactly how necessary are physical touch and bodily engagement for Eucharistic communion? Can online liturgies satisfy the hunger for physicality? Questions like these can spark renewed appreciation for the flesh of the incarnate Christ, or the "carnality" of sacramental presence, as well as fresh engagements with what it means to be human in a digital age.

The Covid-19 pandemic and the restrictions it has generated for physical gatherings have compelled religious communities of all kinds to re-evaluate what constitutes a legitimate religious ritual, or in some Christian communities, a "valid" sacrament. Institutional religious responses to these restrictions have been remarkably diverse, without any consistency even within a single denomination. Many Congregationalist Protestants have been gathering online for Sunday worship via video-conferencing services like Zoom and inviting congregants to gather in front of their computer screens with their own bread and wine as a way to participate "remotely" in a version of the Lord's Supper. Most Roman Catholics, Anglicans, and some Lutheran churches, by contrast, have forbidden "remote consecration" of the Eucharistic elements and have opted for "spiritual communion," a brand of ocular piety in which worshippers view consecrated bread and wine on their computer monitor from home but do not eat anything. This approach is reminiscent of liturgical practice from the high Middle Ages of the kind still practiced in the occasional service of Benediction—*watch but do not touch*.

Among the peculiar religious consequences of the pandemic, we could note the hunger for Eucharist, the depth of which among many Christians is quite striking, and its associated trans-sectarian desire for physical touch and sociality. Some notion of *communion* (however one might define this) would seem essential for human thriving, which perhaps ought to feature more prominently in foundational theologies that seek to articulate what it means to be human at all. This might prompt, in turn, a kind of reassessment of what is arguably *the* doctrinal touchstone for a Christian orthodoxy: the incarnation of the Divine Word in human flesh.

Two overlapping spheres of technology development offer helpful framing when trying to parse the various meanings of "human" in theological vocabularies, especially in light of the Eucharistic quandaries posed by online worship. First, "cybernetics" often stands as an untethered moniker in popular discourse for nearly any kind of human interface with computer technology. The interface is usually presented with either severe limitations (these support human superiority over technology devices) or with alarm (the risk of subverting the genuinely human with "unhuman" technologies). The television series *Star Trek: The Next Generation* illustrates both of these approaches to the human/computer conjunction: with respect to the first, the recurring character of Lt. Commander Data is an android who in nearly every respect appears superior to biological humans except that he lacks emotions (depending on the storyline of a given episode, this lack can seem a welcome respite from emotional turmoil but it mostly appears as a significant deficit); and with respect to the second, the greatest threat faced by the humans in this series comes from the "Borg," an alien "race" of cybernetic organisms linked together in hive-like fashion. The term *Borg* clearly evokes the notion of a "cyborg"—and in this case, the dangers inherent to any intertwining of human and computer technology—but also perpetuates a Western cultural fear of Soviet-style Communism in which individuals supposedly disappear into the "Collective" (the name given in the television series to the hive mind of the Borg). This evokes classical liturgical themes concerning Eucharistic participation in the one Body of Christ, especially the status of the individual in relation to that "body."

It's worth noting that "cybernetics" preceded the advent of computer technology by many centuries and derives from an ancient Greek term (*kybernetes*) referring to a rudder or a pilot to guide the course of a boat. It is not merely incidental, in other words, that this Greek word came to describe the role of computer technology in human life. Norbert Wiener first coined the term in 1948 to refer much more broadly to the "study of control and communication in the human animal," but this quickly became associated with the possibility of controlling the human through (computer) technology. Wiener himself expressed concern over how rapidly expanding uses of technology would fall into the hands of those who wish to *control* and not merely aid human endeavours.[1]

Wiener later explored these themes in relation to religion. He noted the vitality of communication technologies for advancing (or deterring) human purposes, which he understood to be intertwined with whatever we mean by "religion," especially in relation to power. "Knowledge," he writes, "is inextricably intertwined with communication, power with control, and the evaluation of human purposes with ethics and the whole normative side of religion."[2] It matters, in other words, that the panoply of technological advances grouped under the banner "cybernetics" originated with reference to *communication* technology. Consider how standard Christian dogmatic theology insists on framing the doctrine of the Incarnation as the *communicatio idiomatum*, or a communication of properties between the human and the divine in the one person of Jesus of Nazareth. The question of whether a "communication of properties" (and this is of course entangled with ancient metaphysics concerning material substances) is a sharing of "essences" (this is usually denied in "orthodox" Christian theology) bears directly on how Christians understand their participation in Eucharistic worship online. What exactly is *communicated* via the Internet? What kind of power enables the communication? Who controls it?

The second of the two overlapping spheres of technology I wish to note here appears in a broad range of futuristic hypotheses grouped under the banner of "transhumanism." The term itself is often traced to Julian Huxley in the mid-twentieth century, who generally embraced rapidly evolving forms of technology as avenues toward overcoming the biological limitations of human existence. Huxley, an evolutionary biologist, worked closely with his brother Aldous, a philosopher and writer known mostly for his novel *Brave New World*, and together they explored the limits of human capacity for progress and how these limits can be transcended. While Julian (whose legacy was tainted by association with eugenics) focused mostly on technology, Aldous tended toward eastern religious traditions and the use of hallucinogenic compounds for enhanced spiritual experience, yet both mark an ongoing quest to ponder the meaning of human life itself in relation to the boundaries of human finitude. R. S. Deese describes this quest with reference to their grandfather, the Victorian biologist Thomas Henry Huxley. The question or problem that underlies all others, according to the elder Huxley, is trying to ascertain the place humanity occupies in nature, including the limits of our ability to control nature, whether nature's power over us is absolute, and so on.[3]

Similar to Wiener's concern with power and control in communications technology, many transhumanists tend to focus their anxiety on the lack of control humans have over our environment. Rather than only "enhancing" human life (telephones, kitchen gadgets, word-processing software) this type of transhumanist seeks to transform and transcend the human condition itself. One among many examples of this possibility is "whole brain emulation," or the uploading of a human being's neural network into a mainframe computer and achieving a form of (digital) immortality. Whether this kind of interface with computer technology is modestly conceived as preserving certain informational patterns (similar to a data archive) or more extravagantly imagined, such as a life-extension technology, enthusiasm for these possibilities currently outpaces technological capabilities, at least according to some.[4] Yet even the possibility of such technology generates an unavoidable question: what is *communion*? Unavoidable, because one of the first quandaries one might confront in the process of whole brain emulation is whether anyone else can join us in that digital environment. If so, what would it mean to be "in relation" with them apart from physical bodies? Christian churches are pondering the same line of questioning as they confront the restrictions imposed on worship by the Covid-19 pandemic.

Pondering Eucharistic theologies in relation to these technology sectors suggests two interrelated areas of theological investigation. First, "physical reality" now stands as a question in relation to "embodiment" and whether these remain intelligible as theological categories in cyberspace. And second, the sociality of Eucharistic practice poses questions about online "gatherings" and what "parts" of us are transmitted digitally. I'll outline both of these areas briefly and then offer some concluding prospects for the possibilities of "cybercommunion" and why the carnality of the "real presence" of Christ still matters, even in a virtual reality.

I Does the (Virtual) Body Provoke Theology?

Womanist theologian M. Shawn Copeland underscores why theological anthropology remains foundational to constructive theological work in Christian traditions. She does this by placing the bodies of women of colour in the United States at the centre of our theological focus. Attending carefully to this intersection of gender and race makes the incarnational character of Christian faith truly matter for material realities. Copeland sets the stage for her approach by declaring that "the body provokes theology." [5] She means bodily life will always resist being captured by textual categories and continually evokes a "something more" about us that is not reducible to flesh but is nonetheless inextricable from it. Significantly for my purposes here, she makes these claims in a book on theological anthropology with the Eucharist as the centrepiece.

Copeland highlights Eucharistic theology for multiple reasons, not least the rite's social character. This matters—is of *material* significance—because of all the ways particular bodies are constrained by the "social body" and especially the forces of empire. Not in spite of these constraints or even distortions, but because of them, Copeland argues that "the body constitutes a site of divine revelation and, thus, a basic human sacrament. In and through embodiment, we human persons grasp and realize our essential freedom through engagement and communion with other embodied selves."[6] Eucharist thus becomes a site not of erasing our bodily differences but embracing them for the sake of discerning our incorporation into the Body of Christ. This leads her to insist that if anyone is missing from the Table, the Body of Christ is incomplete.[7]

I would argue that computer technology compels theological questions about bodily presence along the same urgent trajectory Copeland traces concerning both gender and race. If the body provokes theology, do *virtual* bodies provoke theology in the same way Copeland urges us to suppose? I would argue yes, they do, but not precisely in the same way as the physical body does when in close proximity. Thus the novelty of Copeland's framing for theological anthropology becomes still more complex when we realize that neither physicality nor proximity present self-evident meanings in relation to bodies.

More simply and directly: Are we fully human when we are online? For those who want quickly to answer in the negative, that we are not fully human in virtual space, would they agree that we are *still* fully human when some of our body parts are replaced by pieces of computerized technology, as happens with cardiac pacemakers, neurological stimulators in the brain, and insulin injection pumps in the abdomen? How much of "us" can be replaced by non-organic materials and still leave something that counts as "human"?

These distinctions matter little to most "transhumanists" as they ponder a future that transcends all biological (fleshy) limits on human life. And I find Copeland useful for framing questions like these precisely because of her argument for sacramental inclusion. If excluding anyone from the Table diminishes the Body of Christ itself, then the stakes are rather high in discerning what kind of "bodies" are present when we gather together in online spaces, and what kind of "space" an online worship service creates.

II Can the (Digital) Human Become a Person?

Standard approaches to rehearsing the development of orthodox Christian doctrine tend to stress the differences between ancient anthropologies and modern ones, especially in the West. These differences orbit around the varieties of Greek metaphysics that shaped particular assumptions attached to the substance of bodily life (to which the Divine Word was joined in the Incarnation) and the inherently social character of the human person (which contributed to the ways Trinitarian doctrine developed). Both of these touchstones in early Christian doctrine have surfaced anew today, in a digital environment, and especially, I would argue, in the quandaries over Eucharistic practice online.

Greek Orthodox theologian John D. Zizioulas offers a helpful analysis of these anthropological quandaries, not because he addresses computer technology directly but because such technology highlights the significance of doctrinal debates for ritual formation. In various ways, Zizioulas takes aim at what has been a common target for constructive theological critique for decades—modern Western individualism, and especially notions of *personhood*. He urges us to notice that the elevation of autonomous individuality in the modern West crept into sacramental theology and Eucharistic practice in detrimental ways, what he refers to as the "psychologizing" of the Eucharist. Restricting communion at the Table to an inner disposition and framing it solely as a "vertical" relationship between the individual and God drains Eucharistic practice of what we might call its "bodily sociality." Zizioulas offers the contrasting image of Eucharist as the space where faith, hope, and love are no longer "mine" but become "ours," thus rendering the Table as the path toward God *because* it is the path toward neighbour

> In this way, the human ceases to be an individual and becomes a person, that is to say, a reality which is not a fragment . . . Contemporary humans live every day under the weight of the opposition between the individual and the collective. Their social life is not *communio* but *societas*. And because there is no other choice, their violent reaction against collectivism leads to individualism and *vice versa*: for, paradoxically, the one presupposes the other.[8]

The key insight Zizioulas offers here emerges from the distinction between individuals and persons. "Personhood" is an irreducibly social reality for Eastern traditions in Christian theology and indispensable for articulating the significance of being woven together as members of the one Body of Christ. But would this also mean that personhood is likewise irreducibly *physical*? What would such a claim mean for our engagement with each other online? Can we become persons with each other in a digital milieu? What kind of distance is crossed while my physical body is "presented" to others as reassembled "pixels" of electronic energy on a monitor? Has the whole human person been transmitted across a WiFi network or only bits (bytes) of information?

The current ubiquity of "Eucharistic cyborgs" unsettles what we mean by the "human" in relation to "God," and this might suggest the extent to which these terms have always unsettled common assumptions. Engaging in Eucharist, for example, might forge a path toward whatever is humans are *becoming* but which is not yet determined. This is in part what Zizioulas means when he describes the Eucharist as a form of anthropology, a sacramental portrayal of the human which is necessarily tied to the meaning of "Christ."[9]

This kind of liturgical analysis retrieves the classical arc of Christian theological reflection from the first four centuries in which Christology preceded anthropology; that is, whatever we mean by the "human" cannot be addressed without attending carefully to the Word-made-flesh. Attending to Christ, furthermore, relies on an eschatological frame that precludes any absolute articulation of what has not yet been revealed. After all, the accounts in the canonical Gospels of the post-Easter Jesus tend to destabilize whatever "physical presence" might mean in relation to resurrection.[10] This seems to be the Johannine writer's very point: "Beloved we are God's children now; what we will be has not yet been revealed. What we do know is this: when [Christ] is revealed, we will be like him…" (1 John 3:2). Any questions about sacramental validity in cyberspace would thus need to account for a humanity that is not yet fully knowable.

III Concluding Prospects for "Cybercommunion"

The history of sacramental theology, including the documents of the Second Vatican Council, suggests that the Eucharist will always properly resist categorical definition and stable meanings. This is in large measure because of its eschatological character (or the framing Vatican II provided by describing the church as God's *pilgrim* people). This does not make theological claims impossible but only and always provisional in an evolutionary and eschatological cosmos. Thus, I offer prospects but not conclusions about the meaning of the human in relation to the divine as I bring this essay to a close.

As the Covid-19 pandemic surfaces a profound desire for Eucharistic communion, a mostly novel question has occupied both clergy and laity alike: how important is bodily proximity with each other for recognizing the "real" presence of Christ in the form of bread and wine? Kelly Brown Douglas makes clear why carnality, or the fleshiness of Christian faith matters more generally. Apart from a robust embrace of the physical, bodily existence of human relations, we can slip easily into its dangerous opposite, the kind of demonizing of bodily relations that can fuel the mechanisms of white supremacy. Douglas labels the source for these distressing engagements with bodily relations as "platonized Christianity," or the philosophical equivalent of replacing the actual *body* of Jesus with a suitably sanitized *idea* of Jesus. Detaching that idea from the carnal realities of a particular person makes the idea itself useful for denigrating black bodies as "bestial" in their brutish sexual practices, or nothing more than "Mandingo bucks" and oversexed "Jezebels."[11]

Like M. Shawn Copeland, Douglas identifies as a womanist theologian, an identification at the intersection of gender and race that underscores the socio-political consequences of detaching theological ideas from the carnal realities of flesh-and-blood creatures of God. Thus, the question persists: to what extent does engaging online with others "detach" us from bodily life? Quite likely much less so when we are engaging with each other in both video and audio formats rather than only with textual exchanges, but by exactly how much? When can we say with confidence that an online presence qualifies as "real"? What does *real* have to do with *carnal*?

I want to embrace the possibility that the Internet can communicate something vital of the real presence of Christ without thereby inadvertently endorsing the supposition that online gatherings can entirely replace physically proximate gatherings and risk making the latter irrelevant. In that desire, I am struck by how much these quandaries replicate the debates that shaped the Council of Nicaea and which eventually gave rise to an "orthodoxy" that insists on the carnal character of the body of Jesus—his "realness"—as that with which God communicates certain divine properties.

A whole range of pressing concerns—from digital technology to climate chaos and shrinking habitats—has refreshed the terms of these classical theological debates. The prospects for embracing some form of "cybercommunion," for example, seem analogous in ecologically vital ways to questions about the status and role of other-than-human animals in both theological traditions and liturgical practices. Both areas of concern return to what has animated Christian theology from the beginning:

What does it mean to be human? In recent decades, and not merely coincidentally, that question has been raised in relation to other animals at the very same time as many started raising it in relation to computer technology. We cannot now think the human apart from all other animals (and the ecosystems we share with them) nor can we do so apart from our many technology devices (and the social media they create and make possible for us to populate). Can we think any of this apart from the flesh?

Both other animals and our technology devices prompt reflection on the many inescapable nodes of relation that make us who we are and the ways we describe those identities. Metaphors drawn from the lives of other animals to describe humans, for example, are ubiquitous in human history, whether one is "clever as a fox" or "stubborn as a mule." Not so surprisingly, similar forms of metaphorical speech have appeared in relation to computer technology to describe human forgetfulness ("my hard-drive crashed") or in the other direction, taking metaphors from human life to describe computer behaviour (monitors that "go to sleep").

The Covid-19 pandemic could provide an occasion for noticing in fresh ways how theological ideas interlace with liturgical practices and, in turn, inspire a renewed emphasis on celebrating the Eucharist *eschatologically*: by embracing the unsettled character of what it means to be human beings in relation to each other, to other creatures, and to God. Many Christians have already been pondering such topics without fully realizing it as they struggle with the meaning of *communion* while staring at a computer screen. What will our lives as "Eucharistic cyborgs" mean for our shared engagements with physical spaces and bodily encounters beyond our computers, whether in terms of race or gender or ecosystems? If the presence of Christ can be "real" but not carnal, how will such "reality" shape our interactions with countless other bodies? Could these religious vexations refresh and even enhance our pursuit of communion? I mean "communion" in the widest and deepest senses: communion with each other as humans; communion with other species; communion with the ecosystems of Earth; and *therefore,* communion with God-in-Christ whose own resurrected and glorified humanity remains beyond the current horizon of our understanding. This pandemic, while offering precious few reasons for gratitude, nonetheless highlights communion itself as an eschatological hope, and this could enliven our engagements with whatever the Eucharistic Table might yet mean for the future of our shared humanity.

Notes

1. Norbert Wiener, Cybernetics, *Or Control and Communication in the Animal and the Machine*, New York: John Wiley and Sons, 1948.
2. Norbert Wiener, *God and Golem, Inc.: A Comment on Certain Points Where Cybernetics Impinges on Religion*, Cambridge: The M.I.T. Press, 1964, 3.
3. Richard Samuel Deese, *We are Amphibians: Julian and Aldous Huxley on the Future of Our Species*, Berkeley: The University of California Press, 2015, 2.
4. Ray Kurzweil, director of engineering at Google and author of *The Singularity is Near: When Humans Transcend Biology*, New York: Penguin Books, 2006, belongs among the more enthusiastic and optimistic supporters of WBE, foreseeing the real possibility of "digital immortality" for humans by the year 2045.
5. M. Shawn Copeland, *Enfleshing Freedom: Body, Race, and Being*, Minneapolis: Fortress Press, 2009, 7.
6. Ibid., 8.
7. Ibid., 82.
8. John D. Zizioulas, *The Eucharistic Communion and the World*, London: T&T Clark, 2011,128. See also Andrea Bieler and Louise Schottroff, *The Eucharist: Bodies, Bread, and Resurrection*, Minneapolis: Fortress Press, 2007, 53–56.
9. Ibid., 127.
10. For a compelling treatment of the resurrection appearances in the Gospel accounts for an eschatological anthropology, see Rowan Williams, *Resurrection: Interpreting the Easter Gospel*, London: Darton, Longman, and Todd, 1982, especially chapter 5, "The Risen Body."
11. Kelly Brown Douglas, *What's Faith Got to Do With It? Black Bodies/Christian Souls*, Maryknoll, NY: Orbis Books, 2005, 114.

Notes for an Eulogy on the Finiteness of the Human Condition

RAÚL FORNET - BETANCOURT

Under the generic titles of "posthumanism" and/or "transhumanism" we can presently see widening currents of thought claiming to represent new approaches that go beyond the traditional sense of humanist thinking. While there is no intent to deny the novelty of the challenges represented by such approaches when understanding the human condition, and which can be evidenced, for example through the application of their techniques for the "betterment" of "human material", this article sees these currents alongside one of man's oldest dreams: the achievement of immortality. Against this background we shall argue for the permanence and relevance of man's mortality.

I Should the context initially set out for this contribution be changed?

I have started by posing this question for the following reason:

In the letter inviting me to contribute to this edition of *Concilium* it was stated that it would be dedicated to the consideration of some of the challenges that arise within the specific context of those areas delineated by the posthumanist and/or transhumanist movements and their resonance in various aspects of current day life. The contribution I was asked to make was framed, therefore, within a precise context.

However, during the period between the invitation dated February 2020 and the moment when I began to write this article (May 2020), we found ourselves confronted by an event that has created an entirely new global set of circumstances affecting our present and whose consequences for humanity in the future cannot be determined with any degree of certainty. I refer to the Covid 19 pandemic. Due to this, the planned framework for the contributions to this edition of *Concilium* has alongside it a shadow on the horizon cast on the posthumanist movement. Let me explain myself in a few words:

My impression is that the human experience within the context of the Covid 19 pandemic serves to disprove many of the aspirations that are fundamental in understanding the boundaries of posthumanism – as I shall explain in my second point below. The Covid 19 pandemic has taken humanity "by surprise" as an authentic *tsunami* of its vulnerability. As proof of this you just have to read the continuous opinions in the press to the effect that the pandemic of disease caused by Coronavirus is a global event that has given us back both our sense of our corporeal fragility and a fundamental insecurity in everything we hitherto supposed secure. I consider, therefore, that in light of a situation in which the risks inherent in human life – in spite of the strait jackets imposed specifically to "contain" these "disagreeable" manifestations – make us only too palpably aware of the limits of our finite condition, the visions of the posthumanists are portrayed as no more than illusions reflected in an elitist mirror delegitimised by the drama of ordinary human existence.

In this sense, one could suppose that the experiences of Covid 19 might give us pause for a reconsideration of how contemporary society develops and its horizon of meaning and that this might lead to an inflection point in how we understand and relate to the risks inherent in human existence. Certainly, if there were such a pivot it might diminish the weight of the challenges presented by the posthumanist views that have been proposed as the themes framing this edition. But who could give us the assurance that humanity will make this pivotal change? No one! That is why I said " it might give us pause……" And let me now add that I am talking of a hypothesis that arises, depending on which point of you take, from the humanists' confidence either in the inherent goodness of mankind or in the hope of divine grace; but without being sure that what they suppose or hope might really happen. Because this depends, ultimately, upon the mystery of the conversion of the flesh. This is on the one hand. And, on the other, there is the fact that in the midst of this present pandemic, structural measures are being approved that clearly show that there is a reliance on a return to the old order of things. It would appear that what is on the "agenda" is not about a change of direction aimed at renewal, disrupting the progress of the dominant civilization, but rather its unchanged continuance. This would only serve to demonstrate, yet again, that we humans are "forgetful".

Faced with this probable continuance of a dominant civilization, it makes sense not to change the contextual framework suggested for this contribution. This in no way suggests a giving up on the hope of an about turn of renewal rather than the acceptance that, within the logic of our civilization, one way to respond to the existential crises brought about by the Covid 19 pandemic, might precisely be a reaction of giving greater impetus to transhumanist programmes. Further on, I shall endeavour, as I have said above, to outline the general visions that characterize, in my opinion, the heart of the posthumanist context. This is not about carrying out an analysis of posthumanism, which represents a complex movement and which would call for a separate study.[1] Given the aims for this article some indications on the extent of the hopes that posthumanism offers as a project for the biological betterment of mankind will suffice.[2] This is the aim that is covered in the second point below as an outline of the cultural and social contexts that serve as a backdrop to this article.

II Post humanism": a prospect of new hopes for an ancient human longing

Generally speaking, within the posthumanist movement, what stands out is the significant innovation that their thinking and studies represent as a vision of the future trajectory for mankind. So it is understood that these open up pathways through which mankind can embark upon a "new creation" of self and go beyond the modest limits of the *conditio humana.* And we must accept that, at first sight, this post humanist assessment can seem completely plausible, since it is not drawn from simplistic desires nor science fiction, but is backed up by a structured approach that is already under way as evidenced, for example, in the achievements and advances in the field of biotechnology. But if we take the trouble to expand the perspective of time, turning our gaze towards the cultural history of mankind, and to consider the visions of hope claimed by post humanists as reflected in this mirror, I believe that within this second perspective, we will be able to recognize that this is an innovation which, essentially, resonates to the echo of "human" yearnings that come from long ago.

In making this observation, I do not wish to suggest that the claims of the posthumanists lack innovation. What I do affirm, as the title of this section indicates, is that this is an innovation that has a backstory. Therefore, in consequence: The challenges that come with posthumanism with its vision of new hopes must also be considered against the backdrop of that particular tradition that speaks so much to the "secrets" of mankind, that is to the history of man's desire for immortality, for a life in its plenitude, or at the very least, a life free from pain and illness.

As a representative illustration of this observation on the history behind the posthumanist innovation – and of which we could say that it is as old as the human consciousness of mortality, if we think of the poem of Gilgamesh – mentioning three instances will have to suffice:

1) The image of the human being set out by Julien Offray de La Mettrie
2) The vision of man described as a "prosthetic God" outlined with more than a hint of criticism by Sigmund Freud in writing of man's quest to escape the painful consequences of his risk fraught condition.
3) The prospect of a "human-robot" that would be shaped by the technologies that were being developed around the middle of the twentieth century.

In my opinion, the post humanist project should be seen alongside the history surrounding these three instances; a continuance which would be especially shown through the prolongation of the "mechanistic" impulse that drives these histories and the consequent tendency to describe the human condition in terms that are material and quantifiable, always susceptible of being augmented or improved in the ways in which it operates.

In considering the perspective of the hopeful vision outlined by post humanism, we are faced with a basic challenge which can be summed up as follows: it is the programming for the construction of a (human) reality from which have been expunged the "memories of humanity" that have until now guided us in the identification of ourselves as "human beings", both individually and collectively. Furthermore, although it scarcely needs to be said since it is obvious, it is worth remembering what ensues once this approach makes it clear that posthumanism posits a conception of the human condition according to which it appears, precisely as a consequence of its finite nature, above all as a reality of decay, that is, as a product that bears the inscription of its "expiry date". From there, the apparent "plausibility" of a programme whose orientation is the arresting of decay through repair and thus to stretch out as far as is possible the expiry date of the "human product". This also explains the euphoric way in which the possibilities of increasingly daring interventions in biological inheritance are celebrated, at least by the radical wing of posthumanism to which I allude in this article.

A consideration of this ("anthropological") assumption also allows us to understand that the posthumanist approach's fundamental challenge lies precisely within this programme of a "new creation" for man, given that the technical empowerment and subsequent growth and refinement of the means within reach that have been forecast bring with them a radical inversion in personal terms of what the finiteness of life means.

In order to meet the posthumanist challenge with its expectations of "transhuman" beings, it will be essential to establish whether the pathway foreseen for the technological empowerment of the finite human condition will also signify one towards a life with meaning[3] – the "good life" traditionally talked of by philosophy – or whether, on the contrary, it will rather lead to an increase in a sense of the emptiness of meaning, to the extent that any such technological empowerment might be shown to be either an impoverishment or an improvement in the possibilities for meaning within the lived experience of the finite human condition.

The reflections in my next section suggest that the latter outcome is more likely; in order to do this they set out to show that human finiteness does not need measures of compensation in order to open the door to a life lived to the full.

III For a eulogy for the finite human condition

In his *L´être et le néant*, Sartre, condensed the absurdity of human life as a finite reality in the well known affirmation that the story of a life is the story of a failure.[4] But what is significant for this section is that Sartre made this powerful affirmation on the assumption that it concerned a failure which, although it occurred according to the logic of all finite existence, hurt like an undeserved misfortune within the most intimate part of human beings. And so, I have to ask why the finiteness of life should be so painful. Sartre's answer is also well known: Finiteness hurts like a great misfortune because it is the place where liberty is eaten up by a passion which can never be satisfied: the desire to be like God.[5] I am not going to follow Sartre in his response, although his question as to why the finiteness of human life is so painful as well as the sense in his response that the experience of this finiteness diminishes the fullness of life, does serve me as a stepping-off point.

Sartre and I part company on his observation that finiteness is painful because embedded in it is the sense that a human being feels that there is a "lack" in his experience of being. However, while distancing myself, I do not interpret this experience as a state of disgrace faced with which man has no choice by way of compensation other than to fool himself in desperate acts. (The pursuit of the realisation of the unattainable ideal to which we have already alluded.) I go with the poet César Vallejo rather in interpreting this experience as an awareness by man that finiteness hurts because its "weight" gives rise to the "memorable" sense of expecting something undeserved.[6] Nevertheless: A finiteness that brings to man the sense that his life can have the hope of "something undeserved" is one, far from being a "misfortune", but is a "grace"; it is a finiteness that deserves to be called generous because, although it may be distant and uncertain, to use César Vallejo's metaphor, it wakes within the human condition the hope of a "supper that is not miserable". This finiteness is not destiny; it is a pilgrimage, as Gabriel Marcel has shown in describing the human condition as one that is itinerant.[7]

Seen from this perspective, the condition of finiteness represents a task for man. But this is not a task in the sense that, as transhumanism might suppose, where one's finite condition is made up of the sum of the "defective functions" such as, for example, those of the body, that need to be fixed. I espouse the word task, rather, because both from and within the bounty of finiteness, being human signifies taking on the spiritual struggle of being able to discern the deep roots that enable the lived experience which "hopes for the undeserved" and which is so disconcerting. It is not, therefore, about "repairing" finiteness. It is a task of "preparation", on the way to finiteness, towards understanding that in its makeup, rather than constituting a problem, there beats a "mystery of incitement",[8] which draws us, as Scheler and Levinas have expressed, to follow the footprints of the eternal or infinite in man.[9]

Faced with this point of view, one might possibly and critically observe that it devalues the worth of our finite condition as a temporal existence, in as much as it suggests that its temporality be put to the service of a search for the eternal. In light of this potential criticism, and before we go any further, it is worth stating clearly that the intention points rather in an opposite sense to that of a supposed devaluation: It is the accentuation of the very density of finite human existence, when we consider that it is the possible latency of the eternal that gives finiteness its character of a seminal sense capable of feeling the tension towards the individual that in this, "his" finite time, can never appear as fully realised. It is a question, in other words, of an indication of the tension that it introduces into the lived experience of the finite human condition, to live in the confidence that, " now we are……, and what we will be has not yet been made known", I John 3,2.[10]

From the above it appears that the path to a eulogy for the finiteness of the human condition cannot find its way using those vistas, be they naturalistic or not, that pretend to illuminate the (entire) reality of human finiteness based on the assumption that it is no more than a closed circuit representing the conjunction of a series of risks underpinned solely by mere chance. Because, paraphrasing the unerring methodological approach of Pierre Teilhard de Chardin,11 a eulogy for the finite human condition should also praise, certainly, finiteness and nothing more than finiteness; yet, although this is right, it should do so from a standpoint of encompassing the "entirety" of finiteness. Which means that the eulogy of which I am speaking here needs to seek its orientation in approaches which contemplate finiteness and the constellation to which it can signal its specific manifestations. And in saying this, it should be made clear that the call for a eulogy which attempts to consider "all of finiteness", has nothing to do with yet another quantitative approach, say through an extension of the list of areas to worry about coupled with the sum total of new risks. This claim goes in quite another direction; a direction that, as it has left behind any quantitative vision of the reality of life, follows the path of an intensification of real experiences of man's finite condition with the intention of deepening its internal dimension as the reverse image where it is revealed that these come from "further away" and that, therefore, the root of life needs to be looked for in "another place"..... There is not space in this article to develop the eulogy for man's finiteness from the perspective that has been outlined. So it will suffice, in order to round out these notes, to summarise two eulogies for finiteness that follow the lines set out above. I have selected them from the many possible choices – think of, for example just in the Twentieth Century, Simone Weil, Karl Jaspers or María Zambrano - because they are especially relevant within the context of this edition of Concilium. They are, first material phenomenology with its interpretation of the christian mystery of the incarnation of the "Logos" as a basis of the possibility that the "flesh" of each human being might be a place of theophany.[12] Second, the phenomenology of depression as an ontological expression of the quality of transcendence in finiteness.[13] As a further clarification of my affirmation of its relevance within the context of the theme with which we are dealing, I might be allowed also to add the following: Both approaches, although with differing methods and objectives, highlight the fundamentally revelatory nature of the immanence within the finite human condition, emphasising that man "lives' his rightful state as an "incarnation" of a life that "is appreciated" as a "good inheritance"; and that, consequently, in its carnal state the "warmth" "resonates" of the foundational love that overflows and clears away the supposed frontiers and/or limitations of finiteness. Thus, as an incarnation of life, the finite condition of man counsels us that we should not reduce corporeality to a chance, self-sufficient object, but rather that we live it more as a sacramental reality, or if you prefer, as a reality of a deep rooted tradition that is both transcendental and transcendent.

IV Final reflections

From what I have just observed, I believe it can be understood that my proposition of a eulogy for the finite human condition calls for a deliberate recovery of the concept of interiority for its further development. But this is not interiority in the modern sense of the word which, for the individual conscious of his own autonomy, individualises his finiteness with the express intention of achieving "power" with and over it. His finiteness should be his own work. I am not talking, therefore, of an interiority that, coming from the "desire for power", no longer feels ties that link it either to the heavens or the earth. This interiority, empty of God, of the cosmos and the community is, through its desolate solitude, mute. I am talking of the recovery of the listening interiority of a living being, open to the relationships that conform his finite condition with the constellation. Drawing on San Juan de la Cruz we could call this "sonorous interiority".

Translated by Christopher Lawrence

Notes

1. Drawing on the extensive literature on the subject of post humanism we would cite: Neil Badmington (ed.), *Posthumanism: Readers in Cultural Criticism*, Houndmills: Palgrave, 2000; Ian Chambers, *Culture after Humanism: History, Culture, Subjectivity*, London: Routledge, 2001; Antonio Diéguez, *Transhumanismo. La búsqueda tecnológica del mejoramiento humano*, Barcelona: Editorial Herder, 2017; Bernd Flessner (ed.), *Nach dem Menschen: Der Mythos einer zweiter Schöpfung und das Entstehen einer posthumanen Kultur*, Freiburg: Rombach, 2000; Jesús García Rojo (ed.), *Pensar el hombre. La teología ante los nuevos planteamientos antropológicos*, Salamanca: PPC, 2018; Jürgen Habermas, *Die Zukunft der menschlichen Natur. Auf dem Weg zu einer liberalen Eugenik?*, Frankfurt/M.: Suhrkamp, 2002; Caroline Helmus, *Transhumanismus – der neue (Unter-) Gang des Menschen? Das Menschenbild des Transhumanismus und seine Herausforderung für die Theologische Anthropologie*, Regensburg: Friedrich Pustet, 2020; Stefan Herbbrechter, *Posthumanismus. Eine kritische Einführung*, Darmstadt: Wissenschaftliche Buchgesellschaft, 2009; Oliver Krüger, *Virtualität und Unsterblichkeit: Die Visionen des Posthumanismus*, Freiburg: Rombach Verlag, 2004; Ray Kurzweil, *Homo sapiens*. Leben im 21. Jahrhundert. *Was bleibt vom Menschen?*, Köln: Kiepenheuer & Witsch, 1999; Wolf Singer, *Ein neues Menschenbild. Gespräche über Hirnforschung*, Frankfurt/M.: Suhrkamp, 2003; Enrique Somavilla (ed.), *El transhumanismo en la sociedad actual*, Madrid: Editorial Agustiniana, 2019; Raimar Zons, *Die Zeit des Menschen: Zur Kritik des Posthumanismus*, Frankfurt/M.: Suhrkamp, 2000; and Cary Wolfe, *What is Posthumanism?,* Minnesota: University Press, 2009.
2. It will observed that in regard to post humanism, I specifically focus in this article on the "transhumanist" aspect of this movement.
3. It will be recalled that in the 1930's Freud was already casting doubt on whether the road to technical prosthetics through which man sought to "deify himself" was synonymous with one towards human happiness.
4. Cf. Jean-Paul Sartre, *L'être et le néant*, Paris: Gallimard, 1973, 561.
5. Cf. Jean-Paul Sartre, *L'être et le néant*, Paris: Gallimard, 1973, especialmente 652, 664 y 672.
6. Cf. César Vallejo, "La cena miserable", en César Vallejo, *Los heraldos negros*, Buenos Aires: Losada, 1961, 81.

7. Cf. Gabriel Marcel, *Homo viator*, Paris: Éditions Montaigne, 1963.
8. Emmanuel Mounier, *Introducción a los existencialismos*, Madrid: Ediciones Guadarrama, 1967, 50.
9. Cf. Max Scheler, *vom Ewigen im Menschen*, Berlin: Der Neue Geist Verlag, 1933; and Emmanuel Levinas, *Totalité et Infini. Essai sur l´extériorité*, La Haye-Boston-London: Martinus Nijhoff Publishers, 1980.
10. Also see on this: Jean Guitton, *L´existence Temporel*, Paris: Éditions Universitaires, 1995.
11. Cf. Pierre Teilhard de Chardin, *Le Phènomène humain*, Paris: Éditions du Seuil, 1970.
12. Cf. Michel Henry, *Incarnation. Une philosophie de la chair*, Paris: Éditions Seuil, 2000.
13. Cf. Raúl Fornet-Betancourt, *Con la autoridad de la melancolía*, Aachen: Verlag Mainz, 2019.

Transhumanity, Posthumanity, Anthropocene: Shifting Horizons of Ignorance and Knowledge, Reality and Possibility, Hope and Faith

LEE CORMIE

The whole of Creation is in turmoil, and so are our ways of knowing the world and acting in it. Here I highlight three powerful new discourses of transhumanism, posthumanism, and Anthropocene, for insights into the magnitude of the epochal transitions underway on Planet Earth, increasingly God-like human capacities to act, inevitable leaps of hope and faith tipping the balance toward widely divergent possible futures.

The whole of Creation is in turmoil, and so are our ways of knowing the world and acting in it. Here I highlight three powerful new discourses of transhumanism, posthumanism, and Anthropocene, for insights into the magnitude of the epochal transitions underway on Planet Earth, increasingly God-like human capacities to act, inevitable leaps of hope and faith tipping the balance toward widely divergent possible futures.

> "We know that the whole creation has been groaning in labour pains until now" (Rom 8:22)

Introduction

Since the 1960s waves of progressive social movements have nurtured the voices of the vast majorities of the world's historically marginalized others, in forging critical perspectives on their experiences, sufferings and hopes, revealing previously unrecognised dimensions of life and axes of eco-social (dis)order (capitalist class and world-system, gender and sexual orientation, indigeneity, race and ethnicity, nature). Succeeding generations have developed new waves of critical thinking and praxis (e.g., postcolonial, intersectional, Latin American decolonial, Indigenous decolonial). And in the last two decades other powerful discourses of transhumanism, posthumanism and Anthropocene have become increasingly influential, centring on cascading scientific breakthroughs, new technologies, and expanding human agency. In theological circles we are at the early stages of engagement with these discourses.[1] But, I suggest, they are full of challenges and possibilities. They converge in agreeing on vast changes, fundamentally transforming human nature, society, and (the rest of) nature. Another world is inevitable, it seems, though there is little agreement about which other world, and the place of humans in it, if any.

I Transhumanity

Celebrations of advances in science and technology resulting in capacities to improve nature, including human nature, may sound like science fiction. But prominent experts, government policy makers, university deans, and corporate officers are setting priorities and mobilizing vast resources in making this dream come true, with far-ranging implications for the Earth.

For example, at the dawn of the 21st century the US government's National Science Foundation and Department of Commerce convened a workshop of leading experts from government, academia and the private sector. They were worried about increasing fragmentation within and among scholarly disciplines, increasing costs of economic inefficiency and growing international competition; and they envisioned a new era of unified science closely supported by a reformed education system and linked to the production of new technologies.

And they identified four major clusters of convergence: (a) nanoscience and nanotechnology (manipulation of matter at atomic and molecular scales, leading to applications in medicine, electronics, biomaterials, consumer products, etc.); (b) biotechnology and biomedicine, including genetic engineering; (c) information technology; and (d) cognitive science, including neuroscience. They organized a major project for advancing interdisciplinary, multisectoral dialogue and collaboration over the next twenty years: "Converging Technologies for Improving Human Performance: Nanotechnology, Biotechnology, Information Technology and Cognitive Science" (NBIC). And they published a book with this title describing this project, reporting on trends in key areas, identifying challenges and next steps.

Overall the tone was jubilant. They announced nothing less than the dawn of a new Renaissance in science and technology leading to advances in many areas, like medical technology and health care, and more generally to "tremendous improvement in human abilities, societal outcomes, the nation's productivity, and the quality of life." Indeed, by the end of the 21st century these experts predicted, a new 'golden age' would dawn of "world peace, universal prosperity, and evolution to a higher level of compassion and accomplishment."[2]

Beyond spectacular advances in particular disciplines and technologies, the overall scope and scale of this project is mind-boggling: unifying the sciences; integrating the development of science and technology; establishing research and development priorities; reforming education at every level to prepare people to take advantage of these developments and to contribute to further advances; fostering collaboration among governments, industry, and corporations; organizing projects to address specific issues in many areas; educating the public in appreciating and supporting these initiatives.

And news reports appear daily of amazing progress on many fronts, in agriculture, engineering, manufacturing technologies, communications, most recently in creating vaccines to combat COVID-19. These are truly miraculous advances. And it is difficult to avoid the more general conclusion that they are also fundamentally transforming human nature. As Allenby and Sarewitz point out, concerning global elites in particular who are quick to embrace emerging technologies which help them master the continually shifting techno-human landscape, "[o]f course they are transhuman ..."[3] Many people in the world's middle and upper classes are already living vastly improved, enhanced and longer lives, with new technologies promising to shield them from deepening social divisions and ecological crises, and infinitely expanding the horizons of possibilities in crafting their versions of the good life.

These transhuman realities, though, clash with other important truths about global realities and trends which are largely overlooked in transhumanist discourses, in part because they are based in the natural sciences and technology studies, which largely abstract from the complexities and contradictions of human nature, society and civilization. So far transhumanists' interdisciplinary reach fails to incorporate the critical discourses of the social sciences and humanities referred to above. They too overlook the impacts of colossal concentrations of wealth and power in shaping/mis-shaping the dynamics of social order and change along the axes of class, race, gender, and homocentrism vis-a-vis (the rest of) nature. They fail to consider continuing resistance in cascading waves of social justice, eco-justice, etc. movements, and the sparks of hope for a different future.

They overlook too the impacts of wealth and power in establishing research and development priorities and strategies in the development of nanoscience and technology. In epistemological terms, transhumanist discourses reinscribe naive positivist views of science as a purely innocent force, neutral, value free, objective, universally applicable, and of technology as purely neutral, able to be used for good or ill. They conveniently overlook the sordid history of government, military, and corporate interests in obstructing/misusing/distorting research and development in particular areas, and in skewing overall research priorities and directions (e.g., denial industries distorting public awareness of the risks related to toxic chemicals, nuclear energy, tobacco, climate change). In these respects, transhumanist discourses resemble blind faith in science and technology more than following the Spirit with an open, critical, ever-questioning and provisional faith.

II Posthumanity

There is no hard boundary between transhumanist and posthumanist perspectives. Here I use the term posthumanist to signify discourses pointing beyond piecemeal improvements, to the qualitative expansion and enhancement of human functioning, e.g., to the transcendence of earlier expressions of human nature.

As one pioneering figure, Nick Bostrom, defines it, this is an interdisciplinary approach focusing on the sustained enhancement of the human condition using technologies, like genetic engineering, information technology and artificial intelligence. In this view, "human nature is a work in progress," which this generation of humans is learning to "remold in desirable ways." The goal includes "radical extension of human health-span, eradication of disease, elimination of unnecessary suffering, and augmentation of human intellectual, physical, and emotional capacities," along with "economic, social, institutional designs, cultural development, and psychological skills and techniques." Ultimately, these pioneers hope, "by responsible use of science, technology, and other rational means we shall eventually manage to become post-human, beings with vastly greater capacities than present human beings have."[4]

In the same spirit, other influential scientists point to an even more wondrous future. "By 2100," physicist Michio Kaku foresees, "our destiny is to become like the gods we once worshipped and feared." We are, he proclaims, on the verge of being capable of manipulating objects with the power of our minds, seamlessly linking our minds to computers which will carry out our wishes, of creating "perfect bodies" and extending our life spans. Moreover, we will be creating new "life-forms that have never walked the surface of the earth," and with nano-technologies creating new materials "seemingly almost out of nothing". It is even possible to anticipate harnessing "the limitless energy of the stars," and, having already reached the moon, launching ships into the distant heavens.[5]

Some even imagine a truly cosmic role for humanity in the distant future, able to manipulate the basic laws of nature, even to modify the law of entropy leading to the "big crunch" which astronomers have previously believed is the inevitable outcome of cosmic evolution at the end of time. As Ray Kurzweil, world-renowned leader in the development of artificial intelligence, insists, "the fate of the Universe is a decision yet to be made, one which we will intelligently consider when the time is right."[6]

These are grand visions of a wonderful new golden era. To the uninitiated they may sound like ancient religious doctrines about life in faraway heaven or modern science fiction daydreams with no relevance for the real world. As pointed out above, though, in many political and cultural capitals these visions are woven with the mundane discourses of neoliberal economics and geopolitics in seamless tapestries of progress in which humans become gods and heaven unfolds on earth. Officials in many government, corporate, and university offices are committing great sums to research and development projects along these lines. And the world's middle and upper classes especially are enjoying many good fruits in their personal lives with better health, endless enhancements, increasing longevity, and ever-expanding horizons of personal fulfilment.

On the one hand, then, it is increasingly difficult to avoid the conclusion that human nature and agency are being fundamentally transformed. Some humans do indeed wield God-like powers (mostly for good transhuman prophets generally assume, though some worry about risks and dangers too). As Jackelén observes: "the development toward *techno sapiens* might very well be regarded as a step toward the kingdom of God. What else could we say when the lame walk, the blind see, the deaf hear, and the dead are at least virtually alive?"[7]

On the other hand, as with transhumanist discourses, many concerns and questions remain. Colossal concentrations of wealth and power are overlooked. Naïve faith in science and technology is reaffirmed. Data flooding in from every direction about tipping points, cascading catastrophes, and apocalyptic end times are largely ignored. More generally, it is increasingly clear that once-infallible science is obviously far more limited, and susceptible to narrow self-interests. Alongside great scientific advances confusion and uncertainty are also growing. And many initiatives are underway to reshape the development of science and technology too.

III Anthropocene

Like 'globalization' in the 1980s and 1990s 'Anthropocene' has quickly become an indispensable referent among experts in an expanding range of scholarly disciplines, in popular media, and in the growing range of debates about earth-shaking upheavals and transitions. It was only in 2000, that American biologist Eugene Stoermer and Nobel prize-winning Dutch atmospheric chemist Paul Crutzen, citing their predecessors (including Teilhard de Chardin), introduced the term in geological circles.[8] For those who follow reports of the Intergovernmental Panel on Climate Change much of this is now familiar. It is sobering, though, to realize how broadly, radically and quickly our views of the world and of our places in it have changed, are changing still. For our purposes here, four facets of this rapidly evolving story stand out.

The first concerns the global spread of science centres programs, and research collaboration, setting the stage for the new interdisciplinary, holistic discourse of Earth System science, against the background of expanding study of solar system evolution and still more broadly of the universe.

The second concerns rapidly expanding insight into the earth's major components: atmosphere, lithosphere (rocky outer layer), hydrosphere (water), cryosphere (ice), biosphere (life-supporting zone), pedosphere (soil), and the interactions among them; system and sub-system boundaries and tipping points; and non-linear transitions.

The third concerns the recent conceptualization of the emergence and rapidly accelerating expansion of the technosphere. This encompasses we humans and all our creations, and their interactions with already transformed 'nature' like ploughed and fertilized farmlands, re-routed rivers, and reservoirs, polluted air, land, water, and accompanying energy consumption and prodigious mountains of waste.

And the fourth concerns vastly expanding human agency. Surely the technosphere is a human construction, many features of which were/are deliberately engineered by some humans. Overall, the technosphere far exceeds the capacities of any group(s) of humans to fully understand or to manage, conforming to its own dynamics, like all complex systems marked by accidents and susceptible to chaos and non-linear changes.

Great scientific leaps forward are revealing in ever more detail five previous transitions in Earth history marked by epochal transitions and mass extinctions, including the extinctions of the dinosaurs 66 million years ago. A meteor perhaps 6 miles wide struck the earth in what is today the Yucatán peninsula: creating a massive crater 110 miles wide and 12 miles deep: triggering great shock waves, mega-tsunamis, volcanic eruptions and earthquakes; hurtling pulverized rock and dust into the atmosphere; setting raging fires; creating vast clouds of smoke and debris darkening the sun and abruptly triggering sudden impact winter. And over a longer-term climate disruption, sea level change, changes in the biochemistry of air, land, and water, etc. led to the extinctions of 75% of plant and animal species. And a new world emerged with new spaces for new species to evolve, including mammals in general and homo Sapiens in particular.

Similarly, today, Earth System scientists argue, the sudden appearance and rapid expansion of the technosphere is triggering nothing less than another geological/biological/evolutionary transition in our time, which they propose naming the Anthropocene. This time, though, the dominant species — humans — is also a major actor, who can see what is coming, and, perhaps, change paths before it is too late.

Surprisingly, a few experts interpret these developments as a 'good Anthropocene' with largely beneficial impacts. In the spirit of the technohumanists and posthumanists, they confidently predict that advances in science and technology will make it possible to mitigate the deleterious effects of climate change, to adapt to changing conditions which cannot be avoided, and more generally in the face of great challenges to see creative opportunities.

Most Earth System scientists, though, are terrified at the expanding magnitude of the technosphere and its impacts, which they see as analogous to the impact of the asteroid 66 million years ago in Yucatán, reflected in pollution air, water and land, climate change, biodiversity decline, habitat loss, mass species-wide extinctions. Indeed, a few experts anticipate a quick end to the human-centred epoch, since disrupted planetary conditions will quickly result in reduced human population and impacts, and definitively dispel homocentric illusions of God-like agency and mastery of the Earth. As marine conservation biologist Richard Steiner argues, "[t]he current trajectory of environmental and social decline cannot continue much longer. Indeed, the Anthropocene will be gone in the blink of geologic time."[9]

Again, as with transhumanism and posthumanism, the limits of Anthropocene discourse are quickly becoming clear.

Ironically for a perspective which turns on radical new relationship between humanity and (the rest of) nature, early writings reinscribed the disciplinary gaps among the natural sciences, social sciences and the humanities. Like the discourses of transhumanism and posthumanism they overlooked the insights, concerns and questions of critical activists and scholars since the 1960s. And these 'social' matters are pivotal in defining the Anthropocene and dating it beginning.

For geologists, designation of a new epoch requires hard geological evidence in the sedimentary record. Some scholars point to the use of fire by early humans, or the invention of agriculture, or the inventions of cities and civilization, or the first wave of globalization in the 16th and 17th centuries setting the stage for the emergence of the modern/colonial capitalist world system, or the industrial revolution in Europe in the 18th century. But these dates, while significant, are not reflected in a distinctive marker, a 'golden spike', in the fossil record providing evidence of abrupt, massive, worldwide changes.

But there are markers that fit these requirements. And support is rapidly growing for a date around 1950, with the sudden appearance in sedimentary layers around the world around the world of radioactive particles from new nuclear weapons era, beginning with the US's dropping atom bombs on Hiroshima and Nagasaki in 1945 and nuclear weapons testing. Other new techno-fossils first appear in this period, like concrete, plastics, and transformed biology like industrially modified boiler chickens. These were not isolated developments, but products of a large, complex, and evolving global industrial civilization, taking off after World War II in a 'great acceleration.' Clearly, the modern / racialized / gendered / ecologically devastating / militarized / colonial / capitalist world-system is earth-shaking in many ways we are only learning to recognize.

Indeed, senior citizens like me can remember the dawn of the Anthropocene. And, thinking today of my granddaughters and all the children of her generation, it is easy to be overwhelmed, confused, and deeply saddened at the thought that I and so many others had not seen more clearly, noticed soon enough, felt deeply enough, or resisted more strongly. There is much soul-searching to do, and many radical challenges to conversion still ahead.

The good news is that in the swirling winds of epochal change we also have such strong traditions to build on: the recent histories of liberation movements and theologies since the 1960s; the explosions of so many currents of critical thought; indigenous and other traditions which have not succumbed so fully to Western modernity; proliferating progressive social movements like Me Too, Black Lives Matter; and solidarity-building initiatives like the gatherings of activists and critical scholars in forums like World Social Forum since 2001, the World Forum on Theology and Liberation since 2005, and elsewhere.

IV Resurgent Hopes and Faiths

For all the differences among them, I wish to suggest, the discourses of transhumanism, posthumanism and Anthropocene converge in confirming seven fundamental truths at the heart of hope for another future.

1) Less and less of the world is God-given, natural, and inevitable. Rather, Earth with its deeply rooted eco-civilization is unbelievably complex, multi-centred dynamic, violent, chaotic, devolving and evolving, at times in startling non-linear ways, in which accidents and unintended consequences play important roles.

2) More and more of life on Earth is being shaped, and mis-shaped, by human agency (in highly unequal ways), sometimes consciously, most often not, certainly not fully.

3) For all the appropriate emphasis on expanding human agency to God-like proportions we are also witnessing the (re)discovery of the boundaries of human agency, and of realms far exceeding human capacities to understand or influence.

4) There is no single one right discourse weaving together the expanding arrays of traditions, voices, contexts, standpoints and perspectives, traditions, insights and concerns. There is no *pensamiento unico*, no one right way of thinking. The foundations of positivist science formulated at the dawn of European modernity, and still reigning in many centres of power, are crumbling.

5) New epistemological spaces are opening for hope(s) and faith(s). Recognition is growing of the partiality, limitations, and tentativeness of every act of knowing. Experiments with new combinations of tradition, science, popular knowledge, and common sense are proliferating, being tested in practice, reformulated, and renewed.

6) The classic religious/philosophical questions about creation (‘cosmos’, ’universe’, ‘multiverse’), human nature and destiny are again re-opened. In the multiple pressures of epochal transition pushing and pulling us all in different directions, there is no standing still, or going backward. We cannot avoid choosing.

7) Religious communities have much to offer. Of course, no tradition has all the answers to the questions posed by new actors and dynamics in a radically changed and changing world, which require not only doctrinal or theoretical answers, but above all concrete practical answers

for reorganizing our ways of life in communities, societies, and emergent planetary civilization.

But these traditions also offer many stories of apocalypse, of worlds ending and new beginnings. As Indigenous activist and scholar John Mohawk pointed out concerning a Hopi myth of civilizational death and rebirth:

"This story should be thought of not as a fantasy but as a collective memory. The archaeological and geological records show that past civilizations did exist in the desert Southwest [of present-day US], they did decline and disappear, and the people did re-emerge. The story is true."[10]

Let us all pray that Indigenous peoples can inspire us, and that this story of apocalypse/resurrection/rebirth/renewal can be true again.

Notes

1. See Linda Hogan/Michelle Becka/ João Vila-Chã, Technology: Between Apocalypse and Integration, *Concilium* 2019/3.
2. Mihail C. Roco and William Sims Bainbridge, "Overview," in Mihail C. Roco/William Sims Bainbridge (eds.), *Converging Technologies for Improving Human Performance: Nanotechnology, Biotechnology, Information Technology and Cognitive Science*. (Draft report), Arlington, VA. 2002, 1-23, here 3, 6, at http://wtec.org/ConvergingTechnologies/ [16 December 2020].
3. Braden Allenby and Daniel Sarewitz. *The Techno-Human Condition*, Cambridge, MA: MIT Press, 2011, 117-18.
4. Nick Bostrom, Nick. "Human Genetic Enhancements: A Transhumanist Perspective." *Journal of Value Inquiry* 37, no. 4 (2003), 493, at http://www.nickbostrom.com/ethics/genetic.html, [05 July 2020].
5. Michio Kaku, *Physics of the Future: How Science Will Shape Human Destiny and Our Daily Lives by the Year 2100*, New York, NY: Doubleday, 2011, 10-11.
6. Ray Kurzweil, *The Age of Spiritual Machines: When Computers Exceed Human Intelligence*, New York, NY: Penguin Books, 1999, 260.
7. Antje Jackelén, "The Image of God as Techno Sapiens." *Zygon* 37, no. 2 (2002), 293–94.
8. Paul Crutzen and Eugene Stoermer. "The Anthropocene." *International Geosphere-Biosphere Programme Newsletter*, 2000, 41, at http://www.igbp.net/download/18.316f18321323470177580001401/1376383088452/NL41.pdf [8 May 2020].
9. Steiner, Richard. 2017. "From Anthropocene to Ecocene by 2050?" *Huffpost*, 23 October, at https://www.huffingtonpost.com/entry/from-anthropocene-to-ecocene-by-2050_us_59e7b66ce4b0e60c4aa3678c, [18 May 2020].
10. John Mohawk, "Surviving Hard Times: It's not for Sissies." *Yes Magazine*, Summer 2006, at Http://www.yesmagazine.org/article.asp?ID=1466 [6 July 2020).

Artificial Intelligence: Angel Machines for Posthuman Times?

H. S. WILSON

With the relentless progress in digital, bio-technologies, and robots with artificial Intelligence, humans are destined to live with machines they have invented. It is projected that AI with superhuman capacities may soon be ushering a posthuman era. Communities, governments and international organizations are concerned about regulating the use of AI. Cognizance of the devastation caused by dropping nuclear bombs on Hiroshima and Nagasaki, the collective human efforts have prevented such destructive use of nuclear bombs so far. Similar collective effort, especially the help of Christian theology must be organized in dealing with AI to assure the needed protection for humanity and all life.

I Present trend: Angels to machine

When I was growing up, Sunday School teachers told us that as children we were looked after by guardian angels with power greater than our parents. As adults we were also taught that God keeps constant watch over us, even to the extent of knowing the number of hairs on our head (Luke 12:7). Today humans have come closer to that aspiration through machines with artificial intelligence. For example, the satellite-GPS (Global Positioning System)-, while helping to get to right place, keeps track of the user. Another example is that of a prefabricated home with AI technology offers many desired amenities.

Humans throughout history longed for greater physical power to protect themselves amidst the environmental threats. To overcome, they have tried to comprehend the way nature works and, to harness/imitate the natural forces for their wellbeing. From the making of stone tools tens of thousands of years back, to the digital revolution beginning in the second half of 20th century, humans have progressed towards creating advanced Artificial Intelligence (AI) machines, robots and others in the 21st century with suprahuman capacities. The machines perform similar to humans but with tremendous capacities than an average human being, and even progress beyond it.[1]

This euphoria towards humans and AI machines working together for common good of humanity and life on earth, is metaphorically termed as 'humans and machines dancing together'.[2] With what has been accomplished and the steady inroads of machines/robots powered by AI, Lathan and Ling note that, "A 47-inch humanoid called Pepper, … recognizes faces and basic human emotions and engage in conversation".[3] Thus, humanity is steadily moving ahead from the threshold of transhuman[4] to the possibility of grander posthuman existence.[5] Posthuman existence is a fully evolved world of algorithms, a gradual shift that has already began from organic algorithms (humans) to non-organic algorithms (Artificial Intelligence).

In our day-to-day life, access to computer, laptop, mobile phone, digital camera, internet, iPhone, virtual reality headset, among many other innovations, have given humans tremendous intellectual power that humans previously thought belonged to angels and divine spirits. Humans have not only caught up with the angels but are becoming gods as noted by Yuval Hariri.[6] As per Harari "The upgrading of humans into gods may follow any of three paths: biological engineering, cyborg engineering and engineering of non-organic beings."[7]

A further area of expansion of AI is the Artificial Intelligence of Things (AIoT). The Internet of Things (IOT) include electronic devices being connected through embedded technologies with the possibilities of interacting, sharing data, collaborating as the expected outcome from them. It is predicated that in the coming couple of decades, billions of physical devices will be connected to the internet.[8] In this context the genuine concern is whether the management of world affairs will be shifted from network of communities to network of AIoT.

These contemporary technological inroads in some ways are overwhelming human communities. It is posing challenges to Christian and human-centric worldviews that nourished its followers in the last 2000 years despite numerous encounters from emergent findings in various fields of humanities and sciences. None of the innovations so far has posed a threat to replacing the humans and their domination on their innovations. Therefore, it calls for reassessing the nature and destiny of human life in relation to traditional Christian anthropologies which is also a focus of this issue of *Concilium*. Such an assessment has a bearing on traditional theological themes like creation, sin, salvation, incarnation, Christology/ies, eternal life. At the Christian cultic level, liturgy as a remembered and celebrated repetitive community event needs nuanced innovative liturgical substances and practices. This has implications for appropriate recasting of catechisms, religious education materials, faith and mission statements of Christian communities and theological education.

However, as AI shaped machines projected to take over the hitherto human controlled affairs, challenges humanity to come up with the nature and scope of the 'dance of human and machine'. There is no turning back from the inroads of biotechnological and digital communication innovations penetrating to every aspect of life on earth. Christianity along with Judaism and Islam has a role in the 'nature and scope of dance' as all of them have inherited anthropologies and cosmologies subscribing to humans as supreme creatures in the overall divine plan for life on planet earth.

Through decades of interfaith dialogues, and recent attacks on Islam in the context of ongoing terrorist threats, sections of Christian leaders are in active process of affirming the link between these three religions as Abrahamic family of faith. A recent encouraging outcome was an ecumenical declaration, "A Document on Human Fraternity" cosigned by Pope Francis and Ahmed Al-Tayyeb, the Grand Imam of Al-Azhar in February 2019. Interestingly, the declaration recognizes the positive steps taken in the fields of science, technology, medicine and industry for human good.[9] If this vision is pursued by theologians of the Abrahamic faith family, they will be bound to engage with reality of AI, as they further proceed in dialogue on human destiny vis-à-vis their traditional anthropologies in search of common ground for peaceful existence. This will be an addition to forums such as the John Templeton Foundation Oxford seminars engaging accomplished scientists and leading Christian theologians on the topic of theology in an age of AI. Several Christian scholars are also engaged in reflecting on theology and technology primarily from the that have been ethical perspectives relating to it--"ascending of technoscience as *the* formative cultural factor".[10] Some even aspire for a theology of technology. Such explorations can be assisted by the academic explorations that have been pursued, like on "technological hermeneutics" and "digital hermeneutics".

II Beyond the present

The recognition of the contextual nature of all theologies since 1960s, especially in the so-called Global South countries, meant that understanding theologies as works in progress is an accepted matter. Since the 1960s numerous contextual theologies have emerged seriously engaging with a variety of issues faced by the communities in each location. One of the recent breakthroughs in theology is neurotheology, in understanding human capacity and yearning for the divine. Neurotheology has shifted the seat of religious beliefs from heart to brain, demonstrating the significance and capacity of the brain in human imagination. Therefore, Reza Aslan notes that, "According to cognitive science of religion, religion is first and foremost a neurological phenomenon. …complex electrochemical reactions in the brain".[11] Spirituality is a ubiquitous force in human lives. It is seen as part of human genetics.

The long-inherited legacy of dichotomy between body and spirit is hard to maintain as human body with all its components are operating like a single unit, an electromagnetic field. Jack Fraser notes that "Not only is it *possible* that the human body creates EM fields — it is the only way you can possibly exist as a coherent entity. You *are* an electric field — a giant electric field which holds your atoms together, and which uses other electric fields to talk to other bits of yourself."[12] So, I postulate that when one refers to spiritual, the reference in fact is to human morality, noted as product of evolution of human social life,[13] that is easier to accept/assess than being spiritual. We turn now to important portal of human electromagnetic field, the human brain.

The input from neuroscientists is adding impetus to the probing of still unresolved areas like, what is the evolutionary purpose of religious beliefs, what is the location of the mind, and what is the source of consciousness?

Now that biotechnology is in the process of perfecting the AI that has been possible from the research on the functioning of the brain with billions of neurons and the still-to-be understood way the neurons are connected in the process of reviewing the data they receive and the result they produce for the survival of human life.

From the religious perspectives, it is rational capacity and individual spirit, that marks humans as separate among families of life on our planet. If rational capacity is enhanced through artificial means and the indwelling of spirit is discounted, it raises the question of transcending the limit of human as created and evolved beings.

III Perceived risk and suggested resolutions.

Mark O'Connell notes the possible end result of AI research as follows. "Ultimately, by merging man and machine, science will produce humans who have vastly increased intelligence, strength, and lifespans; a near embodiment of gods."[14] Harari notes the resulting consequential risk as follows: "The seed algorithms may initially be developed by humans but as it grows it follows its own path, going where no humans have gone before—and where no human can follow."[15]

As of now the possible demise of humans, and takeover of the affairs of the world and beyond, by of non-organic-artificial life forms is a distance dream. The immediate consequences of AI technologically enhanced humans are that some human beings acquire yet another means of power that they can use to suppress and oppress those who are denied of that possibility. That possibility calls for drawing on inherited centuries of human efforts towards ethical norms, religious as well as secular, for ideal existence of human and life communities through means of dialogues and consensus in the context of ascending technoscience. To resist any changes or passively accepting consequences are a disservice to humanity.

Taking note of the human tragedy caused by the dropping of the nuclear bombs on Hiroshima and Nagasaki the world communities have done an excellent job so far in containing the further use of nuclear bombs in spite of some world leaders voicing that humanity was at the brink of irretraceable global catastrophe of nuclear warfare especially during the cold war period. So collective human effort has a potential of assuring needed security for humanity.

Besides a number of theologians who have already invested on working on Technology and Theology, concerned politicians, economists, scientists and technologists have been engaged in discerning the ethical concerns that AI has been posing for humanity, and trying to make it a friendly and safe a companion. For example, discourses in World Economic Forums, the conference of Future of Life Institute in Puerto Rico in Jan 2015 and in 2017 at Asilomar, CA. "Asilomar AI Principals" formulated at the conference at Asilomar, CA recommends, that the "The goal of AI research should be to create not undirected intelligence, but beneficial intelligence". The common good as, "Superintelligence should only be developed in the service of widely shared ethical ideals, and for the benefit of all humanity rather than one state or organization".

Further, if AI is going to be completely independent, since it is modelled after the human brain, a self-reflecting and self-regulating organ, David Simpson suggests, why not it be formed as a hero machine, as heroism is a component of human genome. There are humans who risk their lives for complete strangers. So why we cannot build machines focused on superhuman hero intelligence instead of superhuman power intelligence is a live question. For this to happen, Christians will have to work in solidarity with scientists and entrepreneurs engaged in furthering the research on AI to guarantee that at every stage of new innovations the aspect regarding the common good of all life is preserved. As already projected, AI would be a significant asset to accomplish desired "hive mind", "swarm intelligence" "wisdom of the crowd" by harnessing collective wisdom to assist in solving pressing social problems. A possible challenge from the religious perspectives is to make sure that given the cognitive skills and intellectual ability of AI being copied from the human brain, that such copies do not under any circumstances miss out the noble values that humans developed like empathy, honesty, integrity, courage, kindness. That means forming AIs as humans are designed with "emotional and social intelligence."[16]

For Christians, that challenge is to continue to revisit its exclusive claims to truth through special revelation through incarnation of human-divine, son of god, Jesus the Christ, the central core of its faith building on earlier discourses. However, it is a fact that in spite of official teachings of the church on the role and place of Jesus, a number of Christians, people of other living faiths, and those interested, have appropriated the contribution of Jesus to humanity from their own perspectives. So, the challenges of increased use of AI through various gadgets that humanity relies is to accept them as helpful angel-machines. From that perspective, we must re-examine inherited theological themes through the insights of emergent science and technologies to discern segments of realities and religious hypothesis in understanding the nature of human beings, and to overcome the dichotomies, and synchronize the dance of humans and the machines, for better grasp on life and its complexities. This can be done taking seriously into consideration the wisdom proposed by Jaroslav Pelikan that "Tradition is the living faith of the dead, traditionalism is the dead faith of the living."[17]

Notes

1. "The first branch of robot evolution could split between AI and AL-artificial intelligence and artificial life. …trying to recreate life in a synthetic environment—not necessarily something that will look like human. …It assumes that infinite power that humans have (and so can lose) over the machine." Diane Ackerman, *The Human Age. The World Shaped by Us*, New York: WW. Horton and Co, 2014, 210-211.

2. Pratika Gauri "What the Fifth Industrial Revolution is and Why it matters." World Economic Forum. May 16, 2019, *The European Sting. Your Political Newspaper*, 9 April 2020, at https://europeansting.com/2019/05/16/what-the-fifth-industrial-revolution-is-and-why-it-matters/ [22 May 2020]. Whereas Katherine Hayles notes that, "In posthuman, there are no essential differences, absolute demarcations between bodily existence and computer stimulation, cybernetic mechanism and biological organism, robot teleology and human goals". *How we became Posthuman: Virtual bodies in Cybernetics, literature and information*, Chicago: Chicago University Press, 1999, 3.

3. "Worldwide sales of consumer robots…expected to grow …by the end of 2025 with more than 65 million…a year." Corinna E Lathan/Geoffrey Ling, "Social robots play nicely with others" *Scientific American,* (Dec 2019), 30.

4. "Have you ever taken vitamins, antibiotics, vaccinations…? Yes, indeed, everyone is using science and technology to enhance or to alter our body chemistry in order to stay healthy and to be more in control of our lives. We are all transhumanists to varying degrees," Newton Lee, editor, *The Transhumanism Handbook*, Cham, Switzerland: The Springer Nature Switzerland, 2019, 5.

5. "Posthuman has emerged as a way to describe and the growing appreciation for the plasticity and flexibility of 'human nature' spurred by discoveries in biotechnology and virtual information and communication technologies. It functions as an umbrella term, covering a span or related concept, genetically enhanced person, artificial persons or androids, uploaded consciousness, cyborgs, chimeras (mechanical or genetic hybrids). Thus, the posthuman is not any one particular thing; it is an act of projection, of speculation about who we are as human beings and who we might become." Jeanine Thweatt-Bates,

Part Four: Theological Forum

Various Kinds of Priests

PAUL M. ZULEHNER

How can the lack of priests that is rife in many regions of the world church be overcome without being caught in the celibacy trap? This was what the Amazon synod struggled with and made suggestions about to the pope. He made the decision not to make a decision. This is because his logic of evangelisation demands inculturation, and, thus, synodalisation. The decision will therefore, in the not too distant future, be made in this very context of the Amazon. This will make priesthood more "colourful". As a consequence, in other local churches, too, things will "not remain quiet" (Bischof Franz Josef Bode).

I Liberal and Pastoral Reasoning

The previous discussion about the obligation to remain celibate in the Roman-Catholic Church has shown two dimension which tend to converge. On the one hand there is the modern "liberal" right for a way of life to be determined by the sacrosanct person themselves. In addition, there is a pastoral line of reasoning. The pastoral dimension is connected to more questions: is the eucharist really indispensable for a Christian community, as their source and summit? Is what John Paul II already declared in the title of his eucharist encyclical namely that the church is always being born out of the eucharist (*Ecclesia de eucharistia*, 2003), true? Do those who eat of the body of Christ become His body of sacrifice for the life of the world? Does it thus become a community that serves to change the world, as Benedikt XVI. says with Pierre Teilhard de Chardin? And if this finds agreement: is it not a theologically untenable state that the church does not make it possible for active and live communities of the Gospel to receive the eucharist because it does not have any priests?

II The Amazon synod

With the Amazon synod, the discussion has reached a new climax. It is no longer protesting reform groups, but a clear majority of the bishops assembled in the synod that suggested to the pope that "the relevant authority, within the framework of ‚Lumen gentium' 26 determines such criteria and stipulations for implementation according to which suitable men who are approved by the community can be ordained to the priesthood". (Final document, 111) Those taking part in the synod give "pastoral" reasons: "Many parishes in the Amazon area have enormous difficulty in accessing the eucharist. Sometimes not just months, but years pass before a priest comes into the community again to celebrate the eucharist, to administer the sacrament of reconciliation or the sacrament of the anointing of the sick." (Final document, 111).

The expectation was hight that the pope would take up this suggestion, among those involved in the synod and much further beyond, in areas with an enormous lack of available celibate priests. Had the pope not asked for courageous suggestions to be made to him? Did he not, on the flight back from the World Youth Day in Panama, evidently think that a different form of the priesthood was possible even while making it clear that the model of the celibate priest in the Catholic Church was not up for debate? And, here, too, the pope's reasoning is pastoral: In "very remote areas" it was possible that there was no eucharistic celebration available in communities that were alive and active, which gave rise to a "eucharistic hunger". It was the shepherds who have the holy duty to still this hunger.

In Querida Amazonia, which, first and foremost, applies the encyclical *Laudato Si'* to the ecological challenges of the wounded rain forest and its many indigenous peoples, the pope makes this pastoral way of reasoning his own, ostensibly lifting it to an "official" level: "under the special circumstances of Amazonia, particularly in the tropical rain forest and in the more remote areas, a way has to be found to vouchsafe that priestly service. Lay people can proclaim the Word, they can teach, organise their communities, celebrate some sacraments, develop different forms of expressing popular piety and develop the many gifts with which the Spirit endows them. But they need the celebration of the eucharist as it 'builds the church', and as a consequence of this, a Christian community is 'only built up when it has its roots and its centre in the eucharist'. If we really believe that this is the case, then it is a pressing necessity to prevent this food of new life and the sacrament of reconciliation being withheld from the peoples of the Amazon." (QA 89).

After the publication of the exhortation there was worldwide great enthusiasm about the practical ecology and the pope's appeal to keep the house of the world habitable and to be outraged about those who wreck the world climate (cf. Rev 11,18). At the same time, however, disappointment spread that the pope, waveringly, did not take up the courageous suggestion of the Amazon Synod which he himself had asked for. He does not use the word celibacy even once, but does stress that not all disciplinary questions have to be answered by the magisterium. He did not close a door, but draws attention to the Eucharistic privation and the responsibility of the shepherds. The process is therefore ongoing.

It is possible that he has, in this, done the Church a great, hitherto unrecognised, service with a long term effect. It is conspicuous that the document was not signed in the Vatican, but in the Lateran, the church of the bishop of Rome. A signal to the world church to prepare itself for a new form of exercising the papacy? In addition to this, he takes the conflict with the ideologised opponents to a new level, and explicitly reflects on this process at the end of the document. This, for him, was not about the celibacy of priests, but primarily about the inculturation of the Gospel with the fruit of an Amazonian church that does not lack in anything it needs: a deep interconnectedness with the land and the people and, in addition to that, the preparedness to create, synodally, a rite, a theology and a way of organising church for Amazonia, inclusive of those offices that are needed for the inculturation of the Gospel. Does this include an Amazonian form of the ordo? The pope is encouraging the local shepherds to do their job.

This transformation of how the papacy is executed puts an end to the concept of a lonely pope of the First Vatican Council practically, as much as otherwise – even though it is still very alive in the minds of impatient reformers and even more so in that of ideologised traditionalists, as they do, after all, wish for a pope who makes the decisions (in their favour). The relevance of this is also, and not least, ecumenical. Francis makes reality what John Paul II expressed in the mode of futuristic wishing. Theologians were to start a thought process on a redesign of the papacy which could find ecumenical acceptance. The instrument of this restructuring is called "synodalisation", and thus a decentralising of decision making processes. If this becomes reality, the expectation would no longer be that all due church reforms come from Rome, but often from more peripheral places. Rome makes sure that all changes unfold in line with the Gospel, but also gives encouragement to local development.

If all of this is correct, then it is to be expected that there will be movement in Amazonia soon. The shepherds will pick up the ball passed to them by the pope, find more concrete solutions, present them to the pope, and won't meet any objections. At the same time it is to be expected that, then, "things will not remain quiet" in the world church (according to bishop Franz Josef Bode, deputy president of the German Bishops' Conference on German state television station ARD). There will be more local churches and continental groups of local churches which, with regard to their pastoral situation, will develop and decide solutions. And the pope will not put any obstacles in their way either, but declare their proposals to be legitimate within canon law, and will wish the local churches the spirit of power and prudence in carrying them out.

III On the path to concrete and courageous proposals

When looking for solutions, which will emerge from the regions of the world church that have a blatant lack of priests, in a few short years because of the dramatic speed up because of the ageing of current clergy, some important aspects might be considered.

3.1 The trap of celibacy

Media and church reformers are, without noticing, falling into a "celibacy trap". They overlook many pastorally necessary steps which would have to be taken before the discussion about a development of the (Catholic) ordo makes sense. The demand to quickly ordain married deacons or lay people in church positions are examples of this celibacy trap. It would boost the number of priests, but it would not ensure that the Gospel will still be "sung into" personal lives and the life of society in the future. Priests without Gospel communities are not the solution. Groups that focus on tradition who use this argument are right, even if they base it on different reasons.

The first step is therefore to gather people who are able to, while standing on one leg, tell an atheist the vision that made Jesus trigger a "Kingdom of God" movement in the world. In addition to this, these people are also determined to be part of the Jesus movement and to work within it.

The second step follows naturally from the first: what is needed is a living community of the Gospel which – filled with it to the brim – lives it, tells it to each other, and also celebrates it. They are hospitable communities, open to pilgrims and seekers, which can, as it were, have a temporary taste of the Gospel.

The third thing is that these communities of the Gospel derive their life from the celebration of the Lord's Supper. This, for them, is source and focus, changes violence to love, and makes a community out of those who are celebrating, who take it into their body and em-body it. They are sent forth as washer of feet from this celebration, to change the world in the everyday places of their lives, with people of good will.

It is only with this background that the question arises of who, in such communities of the Gospel, presides over the celebration of the eucharist and who, from its depth, fulfils the main duty for the community they are entrusted with, namely to be liable, in office, for the fact that this community stays on the path of the Gospel and in communion with other communities of the Gospel in the local and the world church. The fact that there should also be missionary ordained people in addition to these community focused ones has not been missed: those who make it their mission not to lead, but to found communities.

The church has always, in the course of its history, had different manifestations of the ordo. This knowledge could remove a lot of pressure from the following predictable development:

3.2 Community founding priests of the conventional kind

The missionary priests who, mostly, win people over for the Gospel and found Gospel communities could reasonably live in celibacy. They need a high theological competence and a sensitive knowledge of culture, because the proclamation of the message they are entrusted with as well as the pastorally needed "spiritual communication" (Karl Gabriel) cannot succeed without it in today's culture. The life form of celibacy makes them flexible, a characteristic that missionaries, female and male, have always had. These missionary priests will come from the "free vocation market". They live within communities because this is probably the only way to live celibacy with dignity and without experiencing isolation in this de-networked modern culture.

One side note on the celibacy debate might be useful. According to my studies there are only two "high risk ways of living" in modern culture: marriage and celibacy. In both these models, there are people who live well within it. Others "fail". And others live in manifold crises. To carry out a pastoral task well, however, contented people are needed. This is why discontent people in celibacy and discontent married people face large obstacles in carrying out a pastoral function. This is why it would be useful not to have a discussion about different ways of living a life, but about life contentment regardless of the chosen path. This even suggests that the choice of a way of life should be changed if the contentment with life can not blossom again in the current one despite much effort. Or are there people who are not happy in any way of life? This would, granted, be an entirely new obstacle to ordination.

3.3 Community leading priests of the new kind

This is different for priests who will serve in the future living communities of the Gospel. They do not come from the free vocation market, but are chosen in living communities. Access criteria are no longer celibacy or academic training. Now, it is rather about the experience that they have gained in communities of the Gospel. They are suggested to the bishop for suitable pastoral and liturgical training and then ordained into a "Team of Elders" (Fritz Lobinger). They work as volunteers, have a secular job, and live within a family.

These two kinds of priesthood would end the pastoral grievance that the eucharist is being scarified on the altar of celibacy.

“Dear Amazon” An Open Window to Integral Ecology and Ecclesial Renewal

GERALDINA CÉSPEDES

In the midst of our planetary circumstances in which the socio-environmental crisis is approaching a point of no return, the apostolic exhortation “Dear Amazon,” which largely collects the Amazonian Synod’s cries and proposals, constitutes an open window to rethink new paths of ecclesial reform and an integral ecology. This article analyses the relevance of the four dreams that, in a prophetic-poetic tone, Pope Francis raises. But some limitations and contradictions are also detected in the document that show a need to hasten other steps in the ecclesial conversion to complete the dream of a Church that attends to the cry and the richness of the indigenous people of the Amazon and the world.

On February 12, the Post-Synodal Apostolic Exhortation “Dear Amazon” (QA) was published, a document in which Pope Francis echoes the main concerns, claims, and proposals that emerged in the process of the Amazonian Synod held in October 2019. The exhortation serves as the official presentation of the Concluding Document of the Amazonian Synod, which is to be taken on and applied by the Church and also serves as an inspiration to all peoples (QA 3-4).

In the midst of our planetary circumstances in which the socio-environmental crisis is approaching a point of no return, QA constitutes a sign of hope and a step forward for a Church that has dared to place the question of the Amazon in the centre of its theological debate and pastoral work. Without doubt, QA is a document of deep significance, insofar as it contains the resonances of a synodal process that had the courage to consult, reflect on and discern crucial issues in today's world (the socio-ecological crisis) and in the life of the Church (the search for new paths of evangelization). The synodal process itself is a sign of hope, a new way of being and making the Church from listening to the people.

To understand the contributions of the exhortation, it must be located within the trajectory of the growing concern of the Church over the last decade for socio-environmental issues. The ecological turn that she has begun to take lately has its focal point in the publication of *Laudato Si* (LS). Without the connection to this encyclical, it is not possible to understand the proposals of the Amazonian Synod and the consequent exhortation of Pope Francis, as well as the concrete steps that, despite the emergence of the COVID-19 pandemic, have been taken to bring into reality the guidelines indicated by the Synod and the exhortation. One of the most important and hopeful achievements to effectively care for the Amazon and its inhabitants is the creation of the Amazonian Ecclesial Conference in June of this year.

I A Church that dreams again

Using the dream genre, Pope Francis, through the presentation of four dreams, gathers with sensitivity, beauty, and delicacy his vision of where the new paths of the Amazonian Church must proceed.

Without forgetting the context of the pandemic in which humanity finds itself, there have been many reactions and comments made about the dreams of Pope Francis in QA. Most of the writings move along the lines of a positive assessment of the document, considering it to be an endorsement of the proposals of the Amazonian Synod and a reaffirmation of the postulates of LS. Other reactions consider that the QA contains three magnificent prophetic dreams of the Church, but that the fourth, which refers to the ecclesial structure is expressed in a strange tone and language, and rather than a dream, it is a nightmare from which one wants to wake.

II Social dream: the rights of the poorest

The connection between the ecological approach and the social question stands out in this first dream. From there, the multiple problems that make up the drama of the Amazon and its inhabitants are described. There is a tone of hope and a positive vision, since the poor are seen not only as victims of the predatory system that destroys flora, fauna, and humanity, but also as protagonists of their own history, as subjects to whom we have to listen, and from whom we have to learn. It is they who have to imagine what their good life and that of their descendants would be like (QA 26).

III Cultural dream: preserve biodiversity

In QA there is a clear vision that the economic system "shamelessly damages human, social, and cultural wealth" (QA 39); the homogenizing tendencies typical of the colonialist and consumerist vision threaten diversity. That is why it is urgent to take care of the human and cultural diversity of the Amazon, its worldviews, wisdom, its way of relating to nature and its sense of community.

IV Ecological dream: guard the Common Home

A typical approach of LS is that the ecological concern is linked to a concern for social problems. This statement runs through QA, especially when presenting the ecological dream, where it emphasizes that "caring for people and caring for ecosystems are inseparable" (QA, 42) The cry of the Amazon is similar to the cry of thc people of God enslaved in Egypt (Exodus 3:7). It is a cry that concerns all of humanity, because from the Amazon we all receive life and we are obliged to take care of it.

We have to learn from indigenous peoples who teach us to contemplate nature, love it, and feel part of it. That is why one of the tasks to cultivate this ecological dream is to awaken "the aesthetic and contemplative sense that God has placed in us" (QA 56). Thus, we will discover in the Amazon a theological place, that is, a place where God shows godself to us and summons us as sons and daughters (QA 57).

An important aspect that QA highlights is that the ecological dream will not come true without the transformation of our habits and lifestyles. For this, it is necessary to incorporate an educational aspect, a pedagogy that helps us to develop new habits. Without a change in people and their lifestyles, there will be no healthy and sustainable ecology (QA 58).

V Ecclesial dream or nightmare? A Church with an Amazonian face

In this section, there are some proposals worth highlighting, such as the emphasis on the need to strengthen an indigenous and well-trained laity; an incarnated and inculturated religious life; the promotion of an itinerant mission and a permanent diaconate of men; the mission of women; the Base Ecclesial Communities (CEBs).

But there are also silences that frustrated the expectations for a transformation of ecclesial structures and ministries, specifically the ordination of married people and the female diaconate, themes of the Conclusions of the Amazonian Synod that were approved by the synod assembly.

What to say about this? It can be interpreted in two ways:

First is to admit that the Church is still afraid to address certain burning issues in which questions of power, tradition, and theological views are at stake. This vision shuts off the possibilities that the Amazonian Synod envisioned and discourages many believers. But, overemphasizing this issue and chaining ourselves to only one aspect of the many pastoral challenges of the mission in the Amazonian territories, can drain our energies and make us forget that the central issue is the Amazon and the defense of the poor.

This does not mean that the ministerial question lacks relevance and urgency, but rather that it needs to be placed in the context in which it was discussed during the synodal process. This must be considered in order to not fall into an exhausting tension between progressives and conservatives, but most of all so that it does not become an issue that displaces the central concern for which the Amazonian Synod was convened and the framework in which it should be raised, a new theology and a new practice of ministeriality.

Second, it is necessary to look for interpretive clues within the same document, as Victor Codina has suggested. In this sense, we see that the issue remains an open window and not a closed door, since Pope Francis himself says that QA does not replace the Concluding Document of the Amazonian Synod. So it is important to understand that one has to obey the proposals of the Amazonian Synod and refer to them to find solutions to the needs and urgencies of the Amazonian territories.

A key issue, not explicitly addressed by the Pope, that should be pointed out, is the need to give continuity to a non-pyramidal-hierarchical, but synodal and participatory way of proceeding, in which decisions are made at the local level and based on community discernment that strongly involves the laity.

This interpretation of the "silence" of the Pope on the ministerial question is much more challenging for the Agents of the Amazon Pastoral, since it supposes they will continue with an attitude of listening to and consulting the Amazonian peoples, and it requires a lot of creativity to promote, not only these two forms of ministerial implications, but also many others that have not yet been glimpsed or mentioned by the Amazonian Synod.

Translated by Thia Cooper

Alterity and Violence in the Americas: The Non-Recognition of Diversity as a Denial of the Communing God

LUCAS CERVIÑO

The covid-19 pandemic revealed distinct widespread evils on a large scale against which the majority of the western population was anaesthetized hunger, inequality, discrimination, and violence. An example of this effect was the wide media coverage of the anti-racist movement *Black Lives Matter,* and the strong support on the parts of sports, cultural, and political figures.

I Increasing interpersonal violence

The increasing racist and ethnic violence or that due to socioeconomic discrimination is a global phenomenon. Violence- be it explicit or implicit, personal or structural, direct or indirect – seems to be the only way, surely the most common, that various social actors have to deal with conflict as a result of their incompatibilities.[1] The "third world war in pieces" (Pope Francis) evidences the violence on the rise, due to the greed and voracity of the reigning capitalist technocratic system that exacerbates the desire to imitate the consumerist lifestyle[2] and promotes a false peace that hides in itself a violent reciprocity.

In many Latin American countries, this violence is the daily experience of indigenous, Afro-descendant, mestizo, popular, and migrant populations due to organized crime, urban inequality, and sexist patriarchy. In Mexico, 60,000 disappeared are ignored and police abuses are constant and visible, with significant social acceptance. In Brazil, more than 75% of those killed by the forces of order are Afro-descendants, but there are no riots.

In Colombia and other countries, the profile of those killed by drug cartels, paramilitary groups, and security forces is male, young, indigenous or Afro-descendant or mestizo. In Chile, the security forces that have sacrificed hundreds of Mapuches have had impunity for decades.

However, it is possible to trace signs of awareness such as the Zapatista movement and municipal self-determination in Mexico, or multisectoral pronouncements that denounce racist policies against Amazonian indigenous peoples, or the Andean women's movement against sexist violence. Activisms that fight against segregation and inequity that determine which lives are worth living and which are not.

II The ruins of the exclusionary models

Conscientization against racial violence is making visible the ruins of exclusionary societies that are based on stigma and contempt for otherness. It shows the limits of multiculturalism: diversity is recognized in official documents, without questioning the real differences, thus configuring first and second class lives.[3] It also raises awareness about the failure of the model of political representation of identities, which ensures freedom for minorities to express their styles and ways of cultural life, but reserving it to the private sphere, without discussing or balancing the imbalance of power and economic, cultural and political resources in the public sphere which are controlled by the same old elites.[4] It denounces the effects of the rupture of the social fabric and the increase in conflict where "there are 'subjects' who are not fully recognized as subjects, and there are 'lives' that are not all – or never are – recognized as lives."[5]

In Latin America, conscientization and social activism, makes visible the deterioration at the base of the social fabric and the crisis of the regulatory institutions and dynamics of society that continue to be traversed by the colonial logic of power, of being, and of knowing:[6] a parallel system of the procurement of justice according to social class or ethnic origin; cultural policies that appeal to a naïve cultural melting pot that makes difference invisible; an economic matrix condemned to extractivist logic and the exportation of raw materials. The bishops in Aparecida denounced "a colonial mentality with respect to indigenous peoples and Afro-Americans [that] still remains in the collective imaginations" (Final approved document, 96).

It is absurd to resign oneself to the fact that the only way to resolve structural injustices and eradicate systemic violence is the dialectical polarization that is moving through our countries. The only result of this path is to increase violence, be it physical or symbolic, psychological or religious, to the detriment of the usual victims.

III Is the communing God violent?

A theological reading of what is described is to connect the roots of intersubjective violence with images of God. What prevents certain Christians from authentically recognizing the egalitarian value of all life expressed differently by indigenous peoples, Afro-descendants, and popular cultures? How is it possible to separate so easily from the evangelical principle of the presence of Jesus Christ in the other (Matthew 25; Luke 10: 29-37)? Is it possible to open paths of faith, hope, and love for an integral liberation of the oppressor and the oppressed, the victim and the victimizer?

The mode of establishing interpersonal relationships reflects our relationship with God. From this beginning, the violence that is the result of unacknowledged alterity shows an incoherence between belief and life in God: the denial of God's communion in everyday life. The centre of the religion is shifted from the Word made Love, which is the relationship to the cultivation or fulfillment of the norm or to action without interiority. This denial of God in practice excludes the nucleus of the revelation: Abba loves each creature and in Christ Jesus opens a dignified and full life to us through the action of the Ruah, the bond of love.

This denial of Abba that hides behind a biased and manipulated Christian practice can be strongly denounced. Belief in God is distorted toward adherence of an idol that justifies and promotes spirals of violence because it feeds on the desire to "find in religion a form of spiritual consumerism tailored to its sickly individualism" (EG 89): sacrifices outsiders in favor of one's own well-being, totalitarian possession of the truth, a feeling of superiority because of a privileged choice that excludes what is different. The mystery of God is encaged by the desires of greed, control, and voracity that feed the current world order. It is a denial in public life of Trinitarian theism (the interpenetration of Abba, Christ Jesus and Ruah) that reveals the fullness of personal and social life as a full, constant, and dynamic interrelation that integrally harmonizes the identity and the otherness of each person with the interpenetration of one in the other.

At the root of Abba's negation are certain theological reflections –more current, institutionalized, and widespread than is believed – that implicitly validate and support the violence that arises from the non-recognition of dignity in otherness. They are theologies incapable of locating their theological work in the immeasurable loving alterity between Abba, the Christ, and the Ruah that avoids reifying otherness.

Perhaps, a way to break the violent reciprocity between people and others with that blurred image of God is to return to the centrality of the Christ event. To relearn to contemplate the crucified-abandoned Christ who is still alive.[7] To contemplate and allow oneself to be contemplated by that fully free act, maximum fidelity, and total gift. To contemplate Christ and to allow oneself to be contemplated from the vulnerability that is the awareness of the insufficiency of gestures and words – including theological ones – to express it. To contemplate it and let oneself be contemplated in the cries of today's victims and of sister-mother earth. To allow oneself to be regenerated by those forgiving victims who, consciously or unconsciously, are configured with the Crucified-Abandoned one in the most radical part of his life: to reconcile humanity with itself, with God, and with other beings.

From contemplating and allowing oneself to be contemplated by this freely given culminating event, non-violent resistance may sprout. This is the path that so many forgiving victims of our time have undertaken out of sheer grace, restoring hope against all hope: the possibility of breaking the vicious cycle of violence with a fundamental act of gratuity and forgiveness. There sprouts faith in a future for everyone in our common home. It is to them that we must return and listen, contemplate their love of extreme gift that is participation in the love of Christ, to babble a theology respectful of the divine mystery that springs from the ruins of the current models of coexistence.

Translated by Thia Cooper

Notes

1. Johan Galtung, *Tras la Violencia, 3R: Reconstrucción, Reconciliación, Resolución*, Bilbao: Gernika Gogoratuz, 1998.
2. René Girard, *Veo a Satán ser como el relámpago*, Barcelona: Anagrama 2002.
3. Alejandro Grimson, *Los límites de la cultura: crítica de las teorías de la identidad*, Buenos Aires: Siglo Veintiuno 2011.
4. George Yúdici, *El recurso de la cultura. Usos de la cultura en la era global*, Barcelona: Gedisa 2002.
5. Judith Butler, *Marcos de guerra. Las vidas lloradas*, Barcelona: Ediciones Paidós 2010, 17.
6. Walter Mignolo, *La idea de América Latina. La herida colonial y la opción decolonial*, Barcelona: Gedisa, 2007.
7. Carlos Mendoza-Álvarez, *Deus ineffabilis. Una teología posmoderna de la revelación del fin de los tiempos*, Barcelona: Herder 2015.

Contributors

ELAINE GRAHAM is Grosvenor Research Professor of Practical Theology at the University of Chester, UK. She is the author of several major books, including *Transforming Practice* (1996); *Representations of the Post-Human* (2002); *Words Made Flesh* (2009); *Between a Rock and a Hard Place: Public Theology in a Post-Secular Age* (2013) and *Apologetics without Apology: speaking of God in a world troubled by religion* (Cascade, 2017).

Address: Department of Theology and Religious Studies, University of Chester, CH1 4BJ, United Kingdom

Email: e.graham@chester.ac.uk.

PHILIP BUTLER is the Assistant Professor of Theology and Black Posthuman Artificial Intelligence Systems at Iliff School of Theology. He is the founder of the Seekr Project, a distinctly Black conversational artificial intelligence with mental health capacities. He is also the author of Black Transhuman Liberation Theology: Spirituality and Technology.

Address: Iliff School of Theology, 2323 E. Iliff Ave. Denver, CO 80210, USA

Email: preed-butler@iliff.edu

STEFAN LORENZ SORGNER is a philosophy professor at John Cabot University in Rome, and author of the following monographs: *Metaphysics without Truth* (Marquette University Press, 2007), *Menschenwürde nach Nietzsche* (WBG, 2010), *Transhumanismus* (Herder, 2016), *Schöner neuer Mensch* (Nicolai, 2018), *Übermensch* (Schwabe, 2019), *On Transhumanism* (Penn State University Press, 2020). In addition, he is Editor-in-Chief and Founding Editor of the *Journal of Posthuman Studies*.

Address: Prof. Dr. Stefan Lorenz Sorgner, John Cabot University, Via della Lungara, 233, 00165 Roma, Italy

HEIDI A CAMPBELL is Professor of Communication at Texas A&M University and director of the *Network for New Media, Religion & Digital Culture Studies*. She is author of numerous articles and books including *When Religion Meets New Media* (Routledge, 2010), *Digital Religion* (Routledge, 2013) and *Networked Theology* (Baker Academic, 2016).

Address: Department of Communication, Texas A&M University 102 Bolton Hall, 4234 TAMU, College Station, TX 77843
Email: heidic@tamu.edu

ANDREA VICINI, S.J., MD, PhD, and STD, is Michael P. Walsh Professor of Bioethics in the Theology Department at Boston College. His research interests and publications include theological bioethics, global public health, new biotechnologies, environmental issues, and fundamental theological ethics.

Address: Boston College, Theology Department, 140 Commonwealth Avenue, Chestnut Hill, MA 02467, USA
Email: andrea.vicini@bc.edu

SUSAN ABRAHAM is VPAA and Dean of Faculty at the Pacific School of Religion, Berkeley, CA.

Address: 1798 Scenic Avenue, Berkeley, CA, 94709
Email address: sabraham@psr.edu

J. JEANINE THWEATT currently serves as academic advisor and adjunct professor in Philosophy and Religion at Flagler College in St. Augustine, FL. She is the author of *Cyborg Selves: A Theological Anthropology of the Posthuman* (2012).

Address: 74 King Street, St. Augustine, FL, 32084
Email: jthweatt@flagler.edu

JAY EMERSON JOHNSON is a priest in the Episcopal Church and a theologian. In summer 2020 he left his position as Professor of Theology and Culture at Pacific School of Religion (Berkeley, CA) to return to fulltime parish ministry in Saugatuck, Michigan.

Address: All Saints' Parish, 252 Grand Street, Saugatuck, MI 49453
Email: rector@allsaintssaugatuck.org

RAÚL FORNET-BETANCOURT – Doctor in Philosophy at Aachen and Salamanca, with "accreditation" at Bremen. Director of the Escuela Internacional de Filosofía Intercultural (Barcelona). Coordinador del Programa de Diálogo Norte-Sur y de los Congresos de Filosofía Intercultural. Recent works: *Para una crítica intercultural de la ciencia hegemónica y Con la autoridad de la melancolí*a.

Address: Kanonenwiese 5 A, D - 52070 Aachen, Germany
Email: raul.fornet@kt.rwth-aachen.de

LEE CORMIE has been a researcher, teacher, writer, and sometime activist concerning liberation theologies and social justice movements since the 1970s in Canada and the US. Currently retired, he taught for over 30 years in the Faculty of Theology, University of St. Michael's College and the Toronto School of Theology.

Address: 11 Marchmount Road, Toronto, ON, Canada, M6G 2A8
Email: lee.cormie@utoronto.ca

H.S. WILSON is the executive director of the Foundation for Theological Education in Southeast Asia. Prior to that he taught at United Theological College, Bangalore, Wartburg Theological Seminary, Iowa, the Lutheran Theological Seminary at Philadelphia and at the Karnataka Theological College Mangalore, India as guest professor.

Address: H.S. Wilson, 140 West Highland Ave, Philadelphia, PA 19118, USA
Email: ftewilson@gmail.com

GERALDINA CÉSPEDES – From the Dominican Republic, she is a nun of the .Misionera Dominica del Rosario. She has a Doctorate in theology from the Pontifical University of Comillas and is a professor in theology in universities in Guatemala, Mexico, and El Salvador. She is co-founder of the Núcleo Mujeres y Teología of Guatemala and a member of the Ameriindia group. She is a on the Board of Directors of the Association of Third World Theologians (ASETT). Her theological and missionary ministry is in the diocese of San Cristóbal de las Casas, Chiapas, México. She has published a varety of writings on liberation theology, spirituality, and ecofeminist theology.

Email: dissgeral@gmail.com

LUCAS CERVIÑO – He is a doctor of fundamental theology and a Bachelor's degree in Missiology. An Argentinian, he lives in Mexico. He investigates interculturality, religious phenomena, and social morality. He teaches at the Institute of Missiology (Bolivia), at the Major Seminary of the Tehuacán diocese (Mexico) and at CEFyT (Argentina).

PAUL M. ZULEHNER, born 1939 in Vienna, is an expert in pastoral theology, research into religion and values. He most recently taught at Vienna University and advised the presidents of the Council of European Bishops' Conferences (CCEE) from 1985-2000.

Address: Kramer-Glöckner-Straße 36, A-1130 Wien (Österreich).
Email: paul.zulehner@univie.ac.at

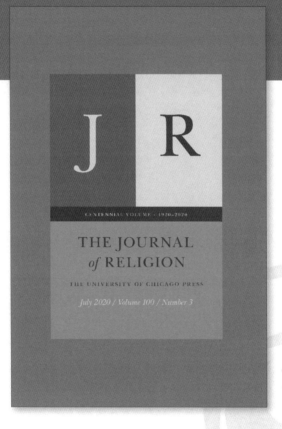

Concilium Subscription Information

October **2021/4:** *Amazons/Congo*

December **2021/5:** *End of Life*

February **2022/1:** *Theology in Asia*

April **2022/2:** *Covid-19*

July **2022/3:** *New Aproaches to the Bible*

New subscribers: to receive the next five issues of Concilium please copy this form, complete it in block capitals and send it with your payment to the address below. Alternatively subscribe online at www.conciliumjournal.co.uk

Please enter my annual subscription for Concilium starting with issue 2021/4.

Individuals
____ £52 UK
____ £75 overseas and (Euro €92, US $110)

Institutions
____ £75 UK
____ £95 overseas and (Euro €120, US $145)

Postage included – airmail for overseas subscribers

Payment Details:
Payment can be made by cheque or credit card.
a. I enclose a cheque for £/$/€ _____ Payable to Hymns Ancient and Modern Ltd
b. To pay by Visa/Mastercard please contact us on +44(0)1603 785911 or go to www.conciliumjournal.co.uk

Contact Details:
Name ....
Address ....
....
Telephone .... E-mail ....

Send your order to *Concilium,* **Hymns Ancient and Modern Ltd**
13a Hellesdon Park Road, Norwich NR6 5DR, UK
E-mail: concilium@hymnsam.co.uk
or order online at www.conciliumjournal.co.uk

Customer service information
All orders must be prepaid. Your subscription will begin with the next issue of Concilium. If you have any queries or require Information about other payment methods, please contact our Customer Services department.

CONCILIUM

International Journal of Theology

PUBLISHERS

Hymns Ancient and Modern, London (United Kingdom)
Echter Verlag, Würzburg (Deutschland),
Editrice Queriniana, Brescia (Italia)
Editorial Verbo Divino, Estella (España)
Editora Vozes, Petrópolis (Brasil)

Concilium Secretariat:
Couvent de l'Annonciation
222 rue du Faubourg Saint-Honoré
75008 – Paris (France)
secretariat.concilium@gmail.com
Executive secretary: Gianluca Montaldi FN